The Church Ladies' Celestial
Suppers & Sensible Advice

D1508392

The Church Ladies' Celestial

Suppers & Sensible Advice

BRENDA RHODES MILLER

AN ELLEN ROLFES BOOK

HP Books

THE BERKLEY PUBLISHING GROUP
Published by the Penguin Group
Penguin Group (USA) Inc.
375 Hudson Street, New York, New York 10014, USA
Penguin Group (Canada), 90 Eglinton Avenue East, Suite 700, Toronto, Ontario M4P 2Y3, Canada
(a division of Pearson Penguin Canada Inc.)
Penguin Books Ltd., 80 Strand, London WC2R 0RL, England
Penguin Group Ireland, 25 St. Stephen's Green, Dublin 2, Ireland (a division of Penguin Books Ltd.)
Penguin Group (Australia), 250 Camberwell Road, Camberwell, Victoria 3124, Australia
(a division of Pearson Australia Group Pty. Ltd.)
Penguin Books India Pvt. Ltd., 11 Community Centre, Panchsheel Park, New Delhi—110 017, India
Penguin Group (NZ), cnr. Airborne and Rosedale Roads, Albany, Auckland 1310, New Zealand
(a division of Pearson New Zealand Ltd.)
Penguin Books (South Africa) (Pty.) Ltd., 24 Sturdee Avenue, Rosebank, Johannesburg 2196,
South Africa
Penguin Books Ltd., Registered Offices: 80 Strand, London WC2R 0RL, England

The recipes contained in this book are to be followed exactly as written. The publisher is not responsible for your specific health or allergy needs that may require medical supervision. The publisher is not responsible for any adverse reactions to the recipes contained in this book.

Copyright © 2004 by Ellen Rolfes Books, Inc., and Brenda Rhodes Miller
Text design by Richard Oriolo
Cover design by Dorothy Wachtenheim
Cover food photos by StockFood
Cover photos by Brenda Rhodes Miller

PRINTING HISTORY
HP hardcover edition / November 2004
HP trade paperback edition / November 2005

HP is a registered trademark of Penguin Group (USA) Inc.

The Library of Congress has cataloged the original HP hardcover as follows

The church ladies' celestial suppers and sensible advice
    p. cm.
   Includes index.
   ISBN 1-55788-437-4
  1. Suppers. 2. Cookery, American. 3. Women—Religious life.
   TX738.C48 2004
   641.5'38—dc22

                               2004052262

PRINTED IN THE UNITED STATES OF AMERICA

10 9 8 7 6 5 4 3 2 1

To Charles T. Rhodes,

a true southern gentleman,

and to

Maria Sara Garcia, siempre.

Acknowledgments

My heartfelt thanks go to all the church ladies who told me their stories or shared recipes and photographs for this book. Their generosity has been incredible.

I appreciate the kindness of Mrs. Martha Chubb and Mrs. Cornell Sharperson, who gave me encouragement and kept me in prayer.

Special thanks go to Ms. Jennifer Bissell, Mrs. Joyce Clemons, Ms. Beverly Crandall, Mrs. Edythe Crump, Mrs. Lolita Cusic, Ms. Dora Finley, Ms. Virginia Fleming, Dr. Joyce Ladner, Mrs. Bessie Samples, Mrs. Melanie Shelwood, Ms. Sharon Robinson, and Mrs. Della Russell for their unselfish support and priceless guidance.

I would also like to thank Bridget Warren, the Friends of the Handley Regional Library, the Afro-American Historical and Genealogical Society, and Ms. Colleen J. Cornell for introducing me to church ladies.

My husband, Rev. Courtenay L. Miller, and my children, Lauren, Jay, and Ben Cooper, deserve prizes for their patience and willingness to listen to "just one more thing." In the midst of their own busy lives, they each found time to help me, as did Dr. Dorothy I. Height, the model for all things gracious.

I am deeply grateful to Ellen Rolfes and Olivia B. Blumer, who are the godmothers of this book. My thanks to Carol Boker, who tested every recipe, gave me ideas for organizing them, and pulled all the pieces together. Thanks also to Judy Kern for doing the final read through and edit.

And dear, dear John Duff, who turned the dream of another "church ladies" book into a reality, will forever be in my prayers.

Love to them all and to those who are now gone but will never be forgotten.

Contents

Foreword

After Thanksgiving dinner last year, Brenda Miller mentioned writing a sequel to her popular cookbook *The Church Ladies' Divine Desserts*. At the time Brenda was thinking about the new book as a guide to good manners, but I suggested that she try a slightly different approach. Rather than producing yet another etiquette guide—of which there seem to be a gracious plenty already in existence—I thought she might consider collecting advice from churchwomen on how to live both decently and well.

A lively discussion ensued, with nearly everyone at dinner offering suggestions on their favorite topics. The depth of feeling expressed by my table companions did not surprise me, but the many lapses of graciousness they described certainly came as a disappointment.

"Please, do write a section on thank-you notes," one guest insisted. "I am so tired of waiting weeks and months on end for a word from the bridal couple or graduate to whom I have sent a gift. It makes me feel bad when I have to call and ask if my gift was actually received."

Then another guest who was a human resources manager chimed in: "It is really sad when people come in for their interview dressed like they're going to a nightclub. Don't they realize what a bad impression that makes?"

"Well, how about when you invite people to an event and they never bother to say whether they're coming or not? Or worse yet, people say they're coming, but they don't show up and they never even bother to apologize?" This comment came from an association manager who hosts dozens of special events every year.

My own pet peeve at the time was the greedy behavior some convention participants display at buffet receptions when light refreshments are served. "You must write about how unseemly it is for women to load up their plates as if they'd never eaten before and may never eat again," I told Brenda. "It just looks so bad. Why, I've even seen women pull aluminum foil and plastic bags from their purses to take food home with them!"

While none of the transgressions we had all observed quite fell into the category of a hanging offense, each was clearly a breach of good manners. We could laugh at the things people did, but regret them at the same time. Living well and living decently seemed to be something beyond the reach of many.

Yet one of the historic roles of the African American church has been to relay, reinforce, and respect good behavior or the way to live decently and live well. It's important, for ex-

ample, for children to learn how they should act during the worship service. By teaching children to sit up straight, to listen, to pay attention, to follow the order of worship, and to observe the many conventions that are a central part of being in church, we prepare them for many other events and activities.

Some churches have abandoned the strict dress codes of the past in an effort to attract people who may have felt excluded by more formal settings, and these days, no one is required to have a full wardrobe of "Sunday-go-to-meeting clothes." Yet every church still has its own culture and norms of behavior and

*Dr. Dorothy I. Height has an elegant hat
for every occasion.*

dress; in short, its own rules for living decently while living well.

And those cultures and norms are most noticeable in the celebrations and ceremonies that are guided by the advice and wisdom of church ladies. From Tom Thumb weddings to Harvest Teas to children's choirs, from Baby Dedications to funerals to church anniversaries, from confirmations to weddings to Sunday School Pageants, it is church ladies who infuse meaning and purpose into these activities.

That is why I so appreciate Brenda's efforts to collect and preserve the examples of church ladies' sensible advice you'll find within these covers. They are a font of wisdom when it comes to advice on how to treat people, how to behave in public settings, what to wear for special occasions, and how to fulfill our responsibilities to one another.

The advice of church ladies is not based on impressing someone else or elevating one person over another. Quite the contrary. The point of good manners and the reason for church ladies' advice is to protect everyone from being made to feel bad by the behavior of anyone else. In a world that sometimes feels out of control, the sensible advice of church ladies can keep us on track.

I hope you enjoy this book as much as I enjoyed my Thanksgiving dinner conversation about it.

Dr. Dorothy I. Height
President Emerita, The National Council of Negro Women

Fourteen Things Church Ladies Often Say

Don't ever mistake my kindness for weakness.

If you lie down with dogs, you will get up with fleas.

You must trust Jesus in order to try Him.

Every whisperer is a liar. Every liar is a thief. Every thief goes to jail.

Don't be iffy about Jesus. He can do anything you need.

Jesus, keep me near the Cross.

He can fix it. Watch and see.

You can't ever put God in a tight (situation) because there is no telling what He'll do.

Wear this world like a loose garment.

You can't beat God giving.

Giving honor to God, who is the author and finisher of my faith.

This too shall pass.

When in doubt, shout.

Blood will tell.

Thanks to Mrs. Illis Smith via Troy Johnston, Rev. and Mrs. Richard Sullivan, Mrs. Johnnie Overton, my mother Carolyn Bolden Rhodes and grandmother Lottie Twyner Rhodes, Joyce Clemons, Rev. and Mrs. George Lyons, and years of listening to church ladies for these sayings.

Introduction

The opportunity to write about church ladies once again is a special and unexpected honor. It has become a rare journey of personal discovery.

Seeking, meeting, and interviewing women of faith all over the country has led me to examine my own beliefs and to understand better the purpose of my life.

These are confusing times. Faith, religion, doctrine, and action seem inextricably bound to politics. Yet the clear example of church ladies living out their beliefs remains a constant.

During the course of writing this book I suffered great loss. The death of a close friend, a surrogate mother, and my own dear daddy in the space of six months was almost more than I could bear.

Every step of the way, church ladies stood beside me in my grief. They have cleaned house for me, laid out my clothes, taken me to the hairdresser, prepared food for the family table, given me refuge, attended to my children, and comforted me and mine in our sorrow.

Church ladies in training: Brenda and Melanie
Grace Rhodes on Easter Sunday circa 1963.

Nothing I have ever done could merit the enormous kindness of the church ladies I've come to know while writing this book, a kindness that closely resembles grace. It is undeserved, it can't be earned, but it is abundant and always freely given.

God bless them all.

Appetizers

If You Can't Judge a Book by Its Cover,
Why Are Those Men's
Magazines on the Newsstand Wrapped in Brown Paper?

CHURCH LADIES' ADVICE ON APPROPRIATE ATTIRE

*I*t goes almost without saying that church ladies have long set the standard on how to dress. Walk into any African American church across the nation on a Sunday morning and you are likely to see row upon row of women attired in fashionable suits or ladylike dresses. Coordinating hats, purses, and shoes are often part of this lovely picture, although these days, in many congregations, the hats are optional.

Even in churches that tend toward a more relaxed style, however, one can't help noticing that there are still quite a few ladies who dress differently for Sunday worship than they do in their everyday lives. Those who might scoff at this insistence on dressing up as a display of wretched vanity or simply pretentious nonsense clearly miss the point.

In the African American church community, attire has always been a way to establish a woman's place and define her identity. From the ornate robes of the choir to the pristine white dresses of the nurses and communion stewards, the severe uniforms of the usher board members, and the elegant outfits of the church ladies in the pews, clothes bespeak the role one plays in the life of the church. And never doubt how much those roles matter.

Yet despite all this emphasis on dress, men, for some mysterious reason, are usually exempt from the scrutiny of the church lady fashion police. Unless, that is, they are men on the young side.

The clothing of teenage boys and young men is fair game for church ladies' comments. Low-slung pants, along with facial hair, braids, cornrows, or any visible hint of a tattoo, are likely to get a rise out of them.

While church ladies may bemoan the way the young men in the congregation choose to dress, they demonstrate by their very example that for them the worship experience demands a certain level of formality. Which means young girls should also beware.

Nothing, and I mean *not one thing,* is more likely to generate more debate among church ladies than what the girls and young women wear to church functions. There is no such thing as a casual discussion on this subject. If you want to arouse a church lady's ire quick, fast, and in a hurry, all it takes is to show up dressed the "wrong way" for a special occasion.

For young girls, the "wrong way" to dress for Sunday worship might include skirts that are tight or very short, along with any article of clothing that is fringed. Tops that cling, bare the midriff, or reveal cleavage are also prime offenders. And God help the girl who comes to church in low-rider pants.

In fact, no matter what the occasion, many church ladies freely express strong opinions on what other women have mistakenly chosen to wear. It may be an off-the-cuff remark or simply a telling glance that alerts the offender to her transgression. Rest assured, however, that somebody will let her know—in the nicest possible way, of course. It can be hard to anticipate when one will cross the line, because the opportunities for missteps are legion. And a lot of these fashion faux pas revolve around how much of the body one can decently show.

Perhaps church ladies seek to protect the virtue of the woman wearing the clothes. Maybe they strive to eliminate temptation from the men viewing the woman. No matter. Something powerful fuels the church ladies' diligent quest for decency.

Some transgressions are fairly obvious. Skintight pants, see-through blouses, halter tops, T-shirts with provocative logos, electrically bright colors, and midriff shirts are all definite no-nos. But what about form-fitting sweater dresses? Open-necked shirts that bare the throat? Sleeveless dresses? Bare legs in the heat of summer? Pants? Short skirts? Dressy high-heeled sandals without hose? Open-toed shoes?

Until a well-meaning church lady has discreetly draped a scarf over your knees in the middle of service, or offered a jacket to cover your bare arms and bosom, you have no idea what it means to be embarrassed. Unfortunately, I do know.

Several years ago—in the middle of one of the hottest summers on record—I accompa-

Church teas were once a source of both fundraising and fun. Most church ladies wore hats and gloves in the 1960s, as did their little girls.

nied my husband to a preaching engagement. Forewarned about the lack of air-conditioning in the church, I wore a lined, sleeveless, yellow linen sheath *with a slip*, sling back pumps *with stockings*, a broad-brimmed straw hat, and gloves. The dress wasn't tight, it wasn't very short, and though my arms and collarbones were uncovered there wasn't even the suggestion of cleavage.

My husband deposited me in a pew and went off to prepare himself for preaching. I sat there for maybe five minutes, fanning myself furiously in the oppressive heat. Then, the elderly church lady sitting next to me pulled from her purse a huge, white, lace-edged rectangle of fabric.

"You can put this over yourself," she said kindly.

"Oh, I'm not chilly. In fact, I'm so hot I may have heatstroke," I answered with a smile, completely missing her point.

She shot me a telling look and repeated, "You can put this over yourself," stretching out each word until I took her meaning.

All About Eggs...Deviled, That Is

No church meal is complete without deviled eggs—hence the several recipes listed here. These four recipes are by no means exhaustive.

Deviled eggs are the perfect finger food—inexpensive and easily dressed up or down, depending on what you add to the basic recipe.

In addition to these recipes, think of adding chopped capers, crabmeat, caviar, shredded smoked salmon and chopped chives, or finely minced country ham, depending on the occasion.

Making picture-perfect deviled eggs is easy. Boil the eggs in anything other than a stainless-steel pot because the eggs will turn it black. Add a pinch of salt or cream of tarter to the water. As soon as the eggs have been at a rolling boil for about four minutes, put a lid on the pot and turn off the heat. The eggs will cook perfectly by the time you assemble your other ingredients, which can be as exotic or as traditional as you choose.

Plunge the cooked eggs in cold water and remove the shells. Don't leave the cooked eggs sitting in water very long because that will cause a dark rim to form around the yolks.

Now that disposable, clear-plastic deviled-egg plates are available, you can safely take several dozen to a church picnic or summer homecoming supper without risking the loss of your special, decorated deviled-egg dish!

Maybe I should have politely rejected her generous offer. Maybe I should have taken a seat somewhere else in the church. Or maybe I should have had the sense just to fall over dead with shame and be done with it.

But I didn't do any of those things. With another smile, I took the scarf she offered and draped it over my offending person. And that was the end of that.

Nothing but Deviled Eggs

This tried-and-true recipe will please the vegetarians at church. If you can't find Creole seasoning, feel free to use seasoned salt or Mrs. Dash seasoning instead.

MAKES 6–8 SERVINGS

8 large hard-cooked eggs
1/4 to 1/2 cup mayonnaise
1/4 teaspoon Creole seasoning, or to taste
Paprika for garnish

Peel the eggs, cut them in half lengthwise, and remove the yolks. In a bowl, blend the mayonnaise and the yolks with a fork until the mixture has the consistency of pudding. Add the Creole seasoning. Spoon the mixture into the egg whites and top with a little paprika. Refrigerate until time to serve.

—Leslie Williams

Everyday Deviled Eggs

It would be hard to find anyone who doesn't like these deviled eggs. To make the eggs extra good, add a little bit of the liquid from the relish to the egg mixture.

MAKES 6–8 SERVINGS

8 large hard-cooked eggs
1/3 to 1/2 cup mayonnaise
3 tablespoons yellow mustard
4 tablespoons sweet pickle relish
Paprika for garnish

Peel the eggs and cut them in half lengthwise. Remove the yolks and place them in a small bowl. Add the mayonnaise, mustard, and rel-ish; mix well. Fill the whites with the mixture. Store in the refrigerator and sprinkle with paprika just before serving.

—Melanie Shelwood

Spicy Deviled Eggs

Even if you swore you'd never eat potted meat, you may find that adding a little bit to these deviled eggs makes them extra tasty.

MAKES 6–8 SERVINGS

8 large hard-cooked eggs
1 (3 ounces) can potted meat (also sold as deviled ham)
1 tablespoon finely minced onion
4–6 tablespoons sour cream
1 teaspoon cayenne pepper

Peel the eggs, cut them in half lengthwise, and remove the yolks. With a fork, blend together half the can of the potted meat, the onion, two tablespoons of the sour cream, and the cayenne pepper. Mash in the egg yolks and add more sour cream if the mixture seems too dry. It should have the consistency of pudding. Spoon the filling into the egg whites and top with a tiny dollop of the remaining potted meat. Refrigerate until ready to serve.

—Brenda Rhodes Miller

Mama's Shrimpy Deviled Eggs

Almost like a shrimp salad, these deviled eggs are very filling and quite delicious. For a "fancier" presentation, cut your eggs in half the short way with a serrated knife to make a decorative egg cup. Then slice a little bit off the rounded end of each half so the cups will stand on the plate without rolling around.

MAKES 8–10 SERVINGS

8 large hard-cooked eggs
¼ cup Durkee Famous Sauce
¼ cup mayonnaise, sour cream, or unflavored yogurt
¼ cup cooked shrimp, peeled, deveined, and finely minced
2 tablespoons finely minced celery
Parsley for garnish

Peel the eggs, cut them in half lengthwise, and set the yolks aside. Finely chop one egg white to add to the yolk mixture. In a small bowl, combine the yolks and chopped egg white with the Durkee sauce, mayonnaise, shrimp, and celery. Fill the egg white halves, garnish with the parsley, and refrigerate until ready to serve.

—*Carolyn Bolden Rhodes*

Deep-Fried Tic-Tac-Toe Xs and Os

To prevent the vegetables from being greasy on the outside and raw on the inside, you want to be sure the oil is deep enough to cover and hot enough to fry them golden brown and crispy. They should rise to the top quickly as they're done.

MAKES 4–6 SERVINGS

1 dozen large mushrooms
1 pound eggplant
Salt
2 large egg yolks
2 ice cubes
Canola oil, for frying
Very fine cornmeal or flour seasoned with salt, garlic powder, onion powder, and black pepper to taste
1 cup ranch or blue cheese dressing

Wipe the mushrooms with a damp cloth and trim the stems to about half an inch. Cut the mushrooms in half so you have two semicircles. Peel the eggplant with a vegetable peeler, and cut it into sticks about 4 inches long and 1 inch wide. Sprinkle with salt and place in a colander to drain. Beat the egg yolks; add the ice cubes, and beat by hand again. Heat the oil in a deep heavy pan or a deep fryer. Dip the mushrooms in the egg and ice mixture. Pat the eggplant sticks dry and do the same. Then dip them both in the flour mixture. Carefully slide the vegetables, one at a time, into the hot oil. Fry until golden brown, remove with a slotted spoon, and drain on newspaper or brown paper covered with double sheets of paper towel. Serve on a platter with the dressing as a dipping sauce.

—Millicent Bolden

Ce

Must-Have Stuffed Mushroom Caps

Thanks to Ms. Joyce Felder's recipe, a new generation now joins the ranks of stuffed-mushroom fans. You will too, once you taste this incredibly delicious double-bite-sized appetizer.

MAKES 10–12 SERVINGS

2 Italian sweet sausages, about ⅓ pound
2 Italian sweet turkey sausages
¼ teaspoon fennel seeds
Pinch or two of red pepper flakes, to taste
½ cup finely minced yellow onion
1 large garlic clove, peeled and minced
Olive oil as necessary
½ cup chopped parsley
½ cup chopped black olives
⅔ cup cream of mushroom soup
Salt and coarsely ground black pepper to taste
30 to 40 large white mushrooms
Shredded Parmesan cheese

Remove the sausage meat from the casings and crumble it in a large skillet. Sauté gently, stirring until the meat is thoroughly done. Add the fennel and red pepper flakes. With a slotted spoon, remove the cooked sausage to a bowl, leaving the rendered fat in the skillet.

Over low heat, cook the onion and garlic in the rendered fat, adding a little olive oil if the pan seems too dry, until the vegetables are tender and golden, about 25 minutes. Remove from the heat. Stir in the chopped parsley and cooked sausage. Stir in the olives and the mushroom soup, mixing thoroughly. Taste and add salt and pepper, if needed. Preheat the oven to 450 degrees. Pull the stems off the mushrooms and wipe the caps with a damp cloth. Fill each cap with the sausage stuffing. Place the caps, stuffing side up, in a lightly oiled baking dish. Sprinkle the tops with Parmesan cheese. Bake 15 minutes or until bubbling and well browned. Let stand 5 minutes before serving.

—Joyce Felder

Ce

Quick-and-Easy Spinach Pie

When you need a quick dish for an afternoon reception, try this recipe. It works equally well as a no-fork appetizer when baked in tiny cocktail pastry shells.

1 pound ground sweet or hot Italian pork
    sausage
½ cup finely chopped green onions
½ cup finely chopped mushrooms
1 (16-ounce) package frozen leaf spinach
1 pound grated Swiss cheese
½ teaspoon ground nutmeg
½ teaspoon salt
½ teaspoon black pepper
1 teaspoon ground sage
1 tablespoon milk, if needed
1 (9-inch) unbaked pie shell

Cook the sausage in a large skillet until brown. Remove the sausage from the skillet with a slotted spoon and drain it on brown paper or paper towels. Leave the rendered fat in the pan, add the onion and mushrooms, and sauté for 4 minutes.

Drop the spinach into 3 quarts of boiling water and cook for 3 minutes. Drain thoroughly and then wrap the spinach in a clean dish towel and squeeze out all the water. Chop the spinach. Preheat the oven to 375 degrees. Mix the spinach and cheese (the mixture will be stringy), add the sausage and seasonings, and mix well. If the mixture seems too dry, add 1 tablespoon of milk.

Prebake the pie shell for 5 minutes, then fill with the spinach mixture and return to the oven for 20 minutes longer, or until the crust is golden brown.

Slice the spinach pie into 1-inch wedges.

—Edythe Crump

Stuffed Collard Greens

Serving collard greens to guests on New Year's Day is a time-honored tradition that guarantees everyone who eats them will have plenty of folding money (greenbacks) during the year. When you fill the greens with a dirty rice mixture, you get an easy-to-eat finger food. This dish is perfect for parties because it looks pretty displayed on a platter and it tastes great. It may seem like a lot of trouble, but it is well worth the effort!

MAKES 20–25 SERVINGS

2 tablespoons vegetable oil
3 cloves garlic, peeled and finely
    chopped
1 pound lean ground beef or lean ground
    turkey
1 (8-ounce) box dirty rice mix
20 large, unblemished collard green leaves
2 (10 ¾-ounce) cans chicken broth
1 medium red bell pepper, sliced in strips for
    garnish
Hot sauce, for dipping (optional)

10 | *The Church Ladies' Celestial Suppers and Sensible Advice*

A Circle of Love

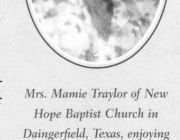

MRS. MAMIE TRAYLOR
NEW HOPE BAPTIST CHURCH
DAINGERFIELD, TEXAS

All her life, Mrs. Mamie Traylor has used her culinary, sewing, and listening skills to create a circle of love and security around her family and friends.

Mrs. Traylor is a lifelong member of New Hope Baptist Church in Daingerfield, Texas, where she is known affectionately as "Mamamie." Although faith most certainly orders her steps, she is not your typical church lady.

Mrs. Mamie Traylor of New Hope Baptist Church in Daingerfield, Texas, enjoying a quiet moment alone.

A seamstress by trade as well as an exceptional cook, she has never been one to join the myriad circles and auxiliaries in her church simply as a way to occupy her time. Consequently, the only circle for her was the New Hope Volunteers, a group of church ladies who care for the sick and anybody else in the community who needs help. A major part of their ministry was then and still is to provide comfort by listening.

At a moment's notice, Mrs. Traylor would cook a meal and bake her delectable 7-up pound cake to share with anyone who looked hungry.

Seniors at the local nursing home were the beneficiaries of slippers she knitted to keep their feet warm and cozy. Quilting was once Mrs. Traylor's favorite hobby, and she never hesitated to share one of her prized quilts with someone who "got chilly at night."

Now that she's ninety-five years old, Mrs. Traylor no longer cooks or sews. But by continuing to be a good listener, her circle of love still cheers the lonely and comforts the sad, as her adult grandchildren will attest.

They bring Mamamie all the secrets of their hearts. She listens attentively and shares her sweet words of wisdom with them. But she never betrays a confidence. When their parents try to pry information out of her, she demurs sweetly, "I don't remember a thing those children tell me. I'm so forgetful now."

I'm willing to bet she winks every time she says it.

Preheat the oven to 350 degrees. Heat the oil in a large skillet and sauté the garlic until golden, being careful not to burn it. Remove the garlic, add the ground meat to the same pan, and cook until browned. Set the cooked meat aside to drain. Cook the rice according to package directions, adding the meat and garlic at the end of the cooking time. Bring a large pot of salted water to a rolling boil. Slide the collard greens into the boiling water a few at a time and cook for no more than 3 minutes. (The goal is to blanch the leaves so they are flexible but still bright green and not fully cooked.) Cool the leaves flat in layers, then cut each one in half, removing the spiny white middle. Put 1 tablespoon dirty rice on each cut leaf. Fold in the sides and then roll the leaf into a small cigar shape. Be sure to fold in the sides so the mixture does not fall out. Repeat until all the leaves are filled. In a baking dish, arrange as many of the leaves as will fit in a single layer and gently pour about 2 inches of chicken broth into the dish. Cover with foil and bake about 15 minutes or until the leaves are the color of an army uniform. You may have to repeat this process, cooking them in batches and adding more broth as necessary. Carefully remove the leaves from the broth with a slotted spoon and set them aside. When all the leaves are done, arrange them on a large platter and top with the red bell pepper strips. Serve the stuffed collard greens with a bowl of hot sauce for dipping, if desired.

—Brenda Rhodes Miller

Open-Faced Mini Reuben Sandwiches

Tiny Reuben sandwiches really hit the spot at parties. While grated Parmesan cheese does not usually go on a Reuben, you'll find that the addition makes for a yummy treat.

MAKES 6–8 SERVINGS

1 loaf sliced party rye bread
¼ cup melted butter
1 cup grated Parmesan cheese
½ cup Thousand Island dressing
½ pound shaved pastrami
1 cup Bavarian sauerkraut with caraway seeds
½ pound Swiss cheese, sliced very thin

Preheat the broiler. Lay the slices of party rye bread on a cookie sheet. Brush the top of each slice with melted butter. Top each slice with grated Parmesan cheese. Layer with pastrami, sauerkraut, Thousand Island dressing, and Swiss cheese, in that order. Broil until the cheese melts, watching carefully so that the sandwiches do not burn. Serve warm.

—Melanie Shelwood

The Body Is a Temple

Mrs. Rubye Smith Bull
St. Augustine Episcopal Church
St. Petersburg, Florida

When you're a church lady who has reached eighty years of age, you've earned the right to offer an opinion on just about anything that strikes your fancy.

Mrs. Rubye Bull recently had surgery on her right knee. Now she uses a cane that one of her daughters had made especially for her, and physical therapy has become part of her regular routine.

In her opinion, walking on a treadmill doesn't hold a candle to natural walking. "The treadmill just pulls you along," she exclaims.

Mrs. Bull knows that God orders her steps even now. She has no doubt that determination counts more than ability and that heart always trumps skill.

Before her knee surgery, she exercised by walking regularly because she believed God gave her a body to use in his service. One of her favorite sayings is, "It is not the haste that wins the race but patience and endurance to the end."

Spoken like a true church lady.

Sassy Party Cheese Straws

Pipe these lovely cheese straws through a pastry bag to make fluted strips or roll the mixture into a log and cut into slices before baking. Either way, the sharp cheesy flavor makes a winner.

MAKES 4 DOZEN

2 cups baking mix (such as Bisquick)
1/2 teaspoon salt
1/2 teaspoon paprika
1 teaspoon cayenne pepper
1/2 teaspoon garlic powder
1/2 teaspoon onion powder
1 pound extra sharp Cheddar cheese, grated
3/4 cup butter, at room temperature

Sift the baking mix and the next 5 ingredients on the list together into a large bowl. Blend in the cheese and butter, mixing thoroughly. Knead well to combine the ingredients. Put the mixture into a pastry bag fitted with a wide fluted tip or roll it into a log and wrap it in plastic. Refrigerate for at least 1 hour. Preheat the oven to 350 degrees. Press the chilled mixture through the tip onto an ungreased cookie sheet and cut off 4-inch strips or slice it into ¼-inch-thick rounds and press the rounds with a fork in a crosshatch pattern. Bake 15 minutes or until golden brown. Remove from the cookie sheet and cool on a rack before serving.

—Mrs. Beulah Hughes

Sardine and Cheese Canapés

Some people laugh at the thought of serving sardines to company. Don't tell them these savory bite-sized treats are made with sardines. Once they get a taste, you can be sure they'll want the recipe. Canned sardines tend to be salty, so don't add any more salt until you've tasted the mixture.

MAKES 8–10 SERVINGS

2 (3.75-ounce) cans sardines packed in oil
  with skin and bones
¼ cup spicy mustard
¼ cup sweet pickle relish
½ cup minced green onions
Garlic powder and black pepper to taste
6–8 slices whole wheat bread, cut into
  squares or triangles
6–8 thin slices of your favorite cheese, cut to
  match the bread

Preheat the broiler. Put the sardines and their oil in a medium bowl and mash with a fork until the sardines, oil, skin, and bones are well mixed. Blend in the mustard, relish, and onions to make a paste. Taste, and then add garlic powder and pepper to taste. Place the bread on a baking sheet, cover with the sardine mixture, and top with cheese. Broil until the cheese melts. Serve hot.

—Wiley L. Bolden

Popeye the Sailor Man's Hot Dip

Corn chips, toast points, or crackers will happily carry this dip from bowl to mouth. If you want to get fancy, you can add crabmeat to the mix, but it is luscious all by itself.

MAKES 8–10 SERVINGS

2 (10 to 12-ounce) boxes frozen chopped
    spinach, thawed
2 (16-ounce) jars Alfredo sauce
1 cup grated Parmesan cheese
Several dashes of hot pepper sauce
1/8 teaspoon ground nutmeg
Salt and pepper to taste
Nacho corn chips, toasted bread cut in
    diamond shapes, or crackers of your
    choice

Drain the spinach in a colander and then
squeeze it in a dish towel to remove as much
water as possible. Chop the spinach finely.
Heat the Alfredo sauce in a medium saucepan,
stir in the spinach, cheese, and hot pepper
sauce, and simmer for 4 to 6 minutes. Add the
nutmeg and heat for 1 minute. Taste, and add
salt and pepper as needed. Serve in a bowl
surrounded by chips, toast points, or crackers.

—Melanie Shelwood

2 (8-ounce) jars cocktail olives stuffed with
    anchovies or almonds
1/2 pound bacon
Toothpicks or skewers

Preheat the oven to 400 degrees. Drain the
liquid from the olives. Cut the bacon into
pieces just long enough to wrap around an
olive. Wrap each olive with bacon and secure
with a toothpick or stick on a skewer. Lay the
skewers on a baking sheet and bake, turning
several times, until the bacon is crisp. Remove
from the skewers (but leave on the toothpicks)
and serve on a small platter.

—Dora Finley

Salty Enough for
Everybody Snacks

**Who doesn't love to gobble up salty snacks? This
easy-to-make appetizer is super-salty and just
about cries out for a cup of sweet, sparkling
Sunday-school punch.**

MAKES 10–15 SERVINGS

David and Goliath
Teeny Tiny Filbert and
Cheese Balls

**Hazelnuts, also known as filberts, usually ap-
pear with chocolate. But they are also delicious
partners to blue cheese. These bite-sized balls
will delight your guests.**

MAKES 12–15 SERVINGS

The Third Quarter
Birthday Month Celebration

MRS. RITA HARDY THOMPSON
NEW REDEEMER BAPTIST CHURCH
WASHINGTON, D.C.

As First Lady of New Redeemer, Mrs. Rita Hardy Thompson has become very attached to wearing hats.

New Redeemer enjoys a tradition of assigning members to quarterly Birthday Clubs that raise money for church projects. Members born in January, February, or March, for example, belong to the First Quarter Birthday Month Club. April, May, or June birthdays go into the Second Quarter Birthday Month Club, and so on. Mrs. Thompson belongs to the Third Quarter group.

Pastor Alan and First Lady Rita Thompson of New Redeemer Baptist Church.

This year, when the church was raising money for the building fund, she hit upon the idea of combining a ladies' luncheon with a hat sale whose profits would go to the fund, and promptly booked the Hat Lady from a local specialty shop, for a Special September Hat Show and Luncheon.

"I printed a flier and about 250 tickets. Everyone born in July, August, or September was asked to sell tickets. Those tickets just flew out the door. As we got closer to the date of the hat show, money started coming in like you wouldn't believe."

She cooked and donated all the food for the buffet meal of peppered chicken, string beans, rice, rolls, and sheet cake. Spinach dips, nuts, and mints were also provided to whet the appetites of the church ladies who came seeking the perfect hat.

"The Hat Lady brought one hundred hats or better, as well as accessories such as men's tie and handkerchief sets, gloves, scarves, and fabulous hatboxes. We set up six tables to display hats in every size, shape, color, style, and variety. Hand mirrors and full-length mirrors let the ladies see how they looked in the hats. We laughed and advised each other on which hats were the most flattering."

Even women who never wore hats found something to catch their fancy at the Hat Show. "A lot of times even hat stores will put your nice new hat in a flimsy box that is just plain cheesy. But our Hat Lady had beautiful heavy boxes with fancy rope closings. Every hat she sold came in its own box. Some ladies who didn't even want to buy a hat couldn't resist buying one of those gorgeous hatboxes."

The fundraiser was a rousing success, and Mrs. Thompson promises that next year's show will even include "big head" hats for people like me who can never manage to find a hat to fit.

I can hardly wait.

½ cup all-purpose flour
¼ teaspoon salt
⅛ teaspoon paprika
⅛ teaspoon cayenne pepper
1 cup butter, at room temperature
1½ cups blue cheese, crumbled
½ cup finely chopped hazelnuts
4 tablespoons water
1 cup blue cheese dressing, in a small bowl

Preheat the oven to 375 degrees. Sift the flour, salt, paprika, and cayenne pepper together into a medium bowl. Beat the butter and blue cheese together in a medium bowl. Add the nuts and flour mixture to the butter and cheese mixture. Stir well and sprinkle with just enough water to form a soft dough. Roll into small balls. Grease a baking sheet with butter. Place the balls on the baking sheet and bake 15 to 20 minutes. Serve on toothpicks with blue cheese dressing for dipping.

—Jacqueline A. Duodu

Holy Ghost Party Meatballs

Many churches now hold "alternative happy hours" on Friday nights complete with nonalcoholic beverages, lively Christian music, and finger foods. These meatballs are the perfect addition to such an event.

MAKES 6½ DOZEN MEATBALLS

1 pound ground beef
1 pound ground pork sausage (hot or maple)
1 cup seasoned bread crumbs
1 large egg, well beaten with ¼ cup soy sauce
¼ cup water
½ cup ketchup
1 tablespoon allspice
1 (1.5-ounce) package spices and seasoning for sloppy joes
2 cups apple jelly
1 cup spicy barbecue sauce

Preheat the oven to 400 degrees. In a large bowl, combine the ground beef, ground pork, bread crumbs, beaten egg, water, ketchup, allspice, and sloppy joe mix. Shape the mixture into small balls. Lay them on a baking sheet and bake for 20 minutes or until well browned. Combine the apple jelly and barbecue sauce and heat in a small saucepan. Place the sauce in a chafing dish, add the cooked meatballs, and serve with toothpicks.

—*Edythe Crump*

Covering All the Bases

Mrs. Geneva Jackson
Zion Baptist Church
Berryville, Virginia

Mrs. Evelyn Thompson displays regal and proper church lady style, including pearls that pass unwritten rules for decorous attire in certain circles.

Mrs. Jackson, a lifelong member of Zion Baptist, enjoys attending Wednesday night Bible study, where church ladies examine and discuss many pressing issues of the day.

One topic recently caused some commotion: Women are not supposed to go to church with their toes or elbows showing. And they should cover their heads and not wear any jewelry either.

The teacher put his students to the test to see how well they embodied those rules. Not one person passed. "I don't go bareheaded to church. I wear a hat every day, but I did have on earrings and my wedding ring," Mrs. Jackson reported.

Asked to explain where the rules originated, the teacher speculated that in days long past a church full of women might have distracted the ministers, who responded by making rules about what women had to keep covered up in order to attend church.

In other words, the rules were designed by ministers to protect themselves, lest they be guilty of looking at women in a shameless way.

Apparently toes, elbows, and hair were quite an attraction back in the day.

Salmon Ball

Any canned meat or fish, be it salmon, shrimp, tuna, chicken, or crab will do for this recipe so long as you adjust the seasoning accordingly.

MAKES ABOUT 3 CUPS

1 (8-ounce) package cream cheese, at room
  temperature
1 tablespoon soy sauce
8 ounces canned seafood or white meat
  chicken
1 tablespoon minced onion
$^1/_2$ tablespoon minced garlic
1 tablespoon minced dill for seafood or
  tarragon for chicken
1 cup finely chopped almonds

Combine all the ingredients in a medium bowl, reserving $^1/_2$ cup of the almonds. Chill for at least 4 hours or overnight. Before serving, place the mixture in plastic wrap and form it into a ball. Roll the ball in the reserved $^1/_2$ cup almonds until covered. Serve with crackers or slices of toasted bread.

—Melanie Shelwood

Ce

The Ham-What-Am Dip

Some people love Spam and others don't. For some mysterious reason, just about everybody has a strong opinion about Spam. Ignore the naysayers and serve this Spam-based dip with dill-flavored flatbread or triangles of rye toast.

MAKES 6–8 SERVINGS

1 (12-ounce) can Spam
1 (8-ounce) container sour cream
1 (2-ounce) package ranch dressing mix
6 green onions, washed

Combine all the ingredients in a blender and pulse until well blended. Transfer to a serving bowl and refrigerate until ready to serve.

—Brenda Rhodes Miller

Ce

This-Little-Piggy-Went-to-Market Bites

Pigs in a blankets, angels on horseback, and other bits of meat or seafood wrapped in pastry or bacon are old faithfuls in the appetizer category. This version adds the jolt of mustard for an easy and unexpected twist.

MAKES 24 SERVINGS

1 (16-ounce) can refrigerated biscuits
1 (16-ounce) package small sausages or
    cocktail franks
1 cup mustard-flavored horseradish or any
    spicy mustard

Separate the biscuit dough into the same number of pieces as you have sausages. Arrange the sausages on a cookie sheet, spread a thin film of mustard on each biscuit piece, and roll the sausages in the biscuit dough. Seal the ends so sausage is covered completely. Bake the dough according to package directions. Serve the piggies with extra mustard on the side for dipping.

—Lauren Cooper

℀

Anchovy Pie in Pastry

A little sliver of this delicious pie goes a long way. If you simply can't bear the taste of anchovies, you can top the pie with minced cooked shrimp or cooked crabmeat flavored with lemon-pepper seasoning.

MAKES 8 SERVINGS

1 (9-inch) frozen deep-dish pie crust
8 small hardboiled eggs, peeled and finely
    chopped
¼ cup mayonnaise
1 cup finely chopped red onion
1 cup ricotta cheese
1 cup sour cream
½ cup finely chopped anchovies,
    cooked minced shrimp, or crabmeat
    flavored with lemon-pepper seasoning
    to taste
Parsley, for garnish
Sprigs of dill, for garnish
Thin wedges of lemon, for garnish

Pierce the bottom of the pie crust with the tines of a fork in several places. Bake it according to package directions and cool completely. Combine the eggs with the mayonnaise in a medium bowl. Spread the egg mixture over the bottom of the baked pie crust. Layer the chopped onion over the egg mixture. In a small bowl, combine the ricotta cheese and the sour cream. Spoon over the onion mixture. Cover and refrigerate overnight. Just before serving, spread the anchovy, shrimp, or crabmeat mixture over the cheese and sour cream mixture. Garnish with the parsley and dill. Serve with the lemon wedges.

—Ellen Robinson

℀

Chicken Log

Use either canned cooked white-meat chicken or a chicken breast you cook yourself for this easy appetizer.

MAKES 8 SERVINGS

2 (8-ounce) packages cream cheese, at room
    temperature
1 tablespoon Worcestershire sauce
1/2 teaspoon curry powder
1 1/2 cups minced cooked chicken breast
1/3 cup minced celery
1/4 cup very finely chopped white currants
4 tablespoons chopped parsley
1/2 cup chopped almonds, toasted
Crackers or party breads

Beat the cream cheese, Worcestershire sauce, and curry powder together in a medium bowl. Stir in the chicken, celery, currants, and 2 tablespoons of the parsley. Refrigerate the remaining parsley. Shape the mixture into an 8- or 9-inch-long log, wrap in plastic, and chill at least 4 hours or overnight. Just before serving, combine the toasted almonds with the remaining 2 tablespoons parsley. Roll the log in the almond/parsley mixture, and serve with a selection of crackers or party breads.

—Joyce Felder

Creole-Style Pickled Herring

Pickled herring can be a bit tart for some folk's taste. Try this recipe and see if your guests don't ask for more.

MAKES 4 SERVINGS

1 (4-ounce) jar pickled herring
2 tablespoons Creole mustard
1/2 tablespoon sugar
3 tablespoons chopped green onions

Drain the liquid from the pickled herring and cut the fish into bite-sized pieces. Combine the mustard and sugar in a small bowl until well blended. Stir in the herring and blend until coated. Toss with the green onions. Refrigerate until ready to serve.

Serve in a small bowl with toothpicks on the side.

—Beverly Crandall

Potted Meat Pinwheels

Dainty pinwheel sandwiches are perfect for cocktails or tea. The hearty flavor of deviled ham with chopped eggs makes a robust and filling pinwheel.

MAKES 8–10 SERVINGS

1 (8-ounce) can deviled ham
1 hardboiled egg, chopped very fine
1 tablespoon mustard
1 tablespoon chili sauce
1/4 teaspoon onion powder
1/4 teaspoon garlic powder
1/8 teaspoon sugar
4 slices white bread

Volunteering Is Like Paying Rent to Live on This Earth

MRS. GENEVA JACKSON
ZION BAPTIST CHURCH
BERRYVILLE, VIRGINIA

What do you call a church lady who is involved in the Extension Homemakers Club and who also volunteers to work in hospice care, with rape victims, AIDS patients, and battered women? A church lady who knits, crochets, does counted cross stitch, and crewel embroidery?

What if this same church lady annually enters more than twenty items in the Clarke County Fair and has won eight best-of-show ribbons? What do you call a church lady who bakes cakes, rolls, and pies, and makes jellies, jams, and chutneys to give as gifts?

If that church lady also serves on the board of several community organizations, was named citizen of the year by her hometown in 1994, and runs her own catering business, you call her Mrs. Geneva Jackson.

According to Colleen J. Cornell, who worked with Mrs. Jackson taking photographs of the Clarke County Fair, her good works are such that she is known throughout the state of Virginia as a true Christian and a great lady.

"I volunteer for everything," says Mrs. Jackson. Although just listening to all her activities is enough to wear out an ordinary person, Mrs. Jackson makes what she does sound easy.

"Once I heard a man say that being a volunteer is like paying rent to live on this earth. I give back, that's what I do now. I give back and I enjoy it."

Mix the deviled ham, eggs, mustard, chili sauce, onion powder, garlic powder, and sugar in a medium bowl. Refrigerate for at least 1 hour. Cut the crusts from the bread. Roll the bread slices flat with a rolling pin. Spread the ham mixture on the bread slices. Roll up the bread slices, and seal the ends with a dab of water. Wrap tightly in waxed paper and refrigerate overnight. Slice with a serrated knife into ½-inch-thick rounds. Arrange the pinwheels on a small platter to serve.

—Candace Grigsby

Hunting Eggs

These are not the kind of eggs children hunt at Easter time but rather a high-protein, high-fat, highly portable survival food known as Scotch eggs that has been transformed into a party dish.

MAKES 9 SERVINGS

1 pound maple-flavored pork sausage
1 pound sage-flavored pork sausage
2 green onions, both white and green
    portions, finely chopped
1 teaspoon summer savory
1 tablespoon fresh cilantro, minced
Dash of nutmeg
2 cups Italian-flavored bread crumbs
9 large hardboiled eggs, peeled and cooled
Vegetable oil, for frying

Mix the sausages, onions, savory, cilantro, and nutmeg in a medium bowl. Pour the bread crumbs into another medium bowl. Divide the sausage mixture into 9 portions. Wrap each egg in sausage mixture, sealing the edges. Roll the eggs in the bread crumbs. Heat about 2 inches of vegetable oil in a deep pot or skillet. Deep-fry the eggs until the sausage is done and the crumbs are golden brown. Drain on brown paper or newspaper covered with sheets of paper towel. To serve, cut each egg in half on the diagonal.

—Ellen Robinson

Star in the East Snacks

Chicken livers, like anchovies, can be an acquired taste. This delicious canapé combines the richness of chicken liver with exotic flavors from the Mediterranean and Far East.

MAKES 8–10 SERVINGS

¼ cup sesame oil
½ cup soy sauce
1 tablespoon hoisin sauce
1 tablespoon finely minced fresh ginger
1 tablespoon finely minced garlic
1 pint chicken livers
6 ounces whole water chestnuts
¼ pound finely sliced prosciutto

In a blender, combine the sesame oil, soy sauce, hoisin sauce, ginger, and garlic. Pulse until well combined. Cut the chicken livers in half and marinate in the mixture overnight. Slice the water chestnuts in half. Drain the chicken livers and make a small slit in each liver half. Insert the water chestnut. Wrap each liver in prosciutto and secure with a toothpick. Broil until cooked through and browned on both sides.

—*Melanie Shelwood*

Cℓℓ

Rosy Red Poppers

What could be more delicious than sweet, ripe cherry tomatoes? Answer: Those same tiny tomatoes stuffed with a filling of your choice. Chicken with just a bit of minced apple or shredded pepper jack cheese mixed with chopped olives would also work well, but I'm partial to the tuna and egg salad filling in this recipe.

MAKES 10–12 SERVINGS

1 pint large, ripe cherry tomatoes
3 hardboiled eggs, peeled and chopped
1 stalk celery, chopped fine
Mayonnaise to taste
Salt and pepper to taste
¼ teaspoon chopped fresh tarragon
½ cup shredded albacore tuna

Wash and dry the cherry tomatoes. Slice off the tops and either squeeze out the innards or remove the pulp with a pointed grapefruit spoon. Combine the eggs with the celery, mayonnaise, salt and pepper, and tarragon. Mix well before adding the tuna and mixing

well again. Taste and correct the seasoning. Spoon the filling into the cherry tomatoes. Refrigerate until ready to serve.

—*Lauren Cooper*

Cℓℓ

Sensational Dip

To earn a permanent spot on any Hospitality Committee, take this dip to a church meeting along with a tray of crisp, raw vegetables.

MAKES 10–12 SERVINGS

1 (8-ounce) package cream cheese, at room
*   temperature*
2 tablespoons sour cream
1 (10-ounce) can tomatoes and green chiles,
*   drained*
¼ cup minced green bell pepper
¼ cup finely minced cilantro
Garlic salt and black pepper to taste

Beat the cream cheese and the sour cream in a medium bowl until smooth.

Stir in the tomatoes, bell pepper, and cilantro. Add garlic salt and pepper as desired. Chill until ready to use. Serve as a dip with grape tomatoes, celery sticks, and baby carrots or your choice of bite-sized raw vegetables.

Cℓℓ

Alternate Sensational Dip

8 ounces Velveeta cheese
4 ounces tomatoes and green chiles, drained
¼ cup finely minced cilantro
¼ cup chopped green onions

Melt the cheese and combine with the tomatoes, cilantro, and onions. Serve hot, as a dip with tortilla chips.

—Millicent Bolden

CHAPTER 2

Breads

Don't Ride a Free Horse to Death Just
Because He's Willing to Run

WHAT CHURCH LADIES SAY ABOUT GRATITUDE

Mrs. Annie Fourth is an elderly church lady well known for her pithy sayings. She has shared her running commentary with her daughter, Joyce Clemons, who contributed the title of this chapter.

The milk of human kindness is one beverage church ladies serve all the time. And sometimes it even comes with fresh-baked cookies. Although every real church lady knows her true reward will come in heaven, that doesn't stop her from looking with approval on people who have the good sense to say thank you right here on earth.

Church ladies certainly bake and cook for church activities, but they also do a whole lot more. They drive elderly members to church and to doctors' appointments, plant flowers, organize special events, and teach Sunday school.

The women of the church prepare baskets for the poor, and they visit the sick, the shut-in, and the imprisoned. They hold clothing drives, establish women's ministries, and run the children's choir.

The children's choir at Warren Street Methodist Church in the 1960s.

Church ladies spearhead neighborhood and church cleanup projects and building fund campaigns. They tithe, raise funds, testify before zoning boards, and organize Vacation Bible School.

Some serve as trustees and administrative officers; others head up Christian Education, Children's Church, or Family Ministries. And they publish the congregation's newsletter along with producing the weekly bulletin, notices in community papers, and fliers for special programs. All these things they do as a matter of course.

Because a church is like a large, extended family, many church ladies make it a practice to give gifts to members of their congregation. They mark birthdays, anniversaries, graduations, weddings, new babies, and new houses with gaily wrapped presents joyously presented.

Any death generates an outpouring of sympathy for family members accompanied by appropriate gifts. Food, flowers, fruit baskets, and cash are often sent to the bereaved as a demonstration of the church ladies' concern.

Sometimes they give presents just because

they love to shop and recognize that buying gifts for other church members is a guilt-free way to indulge their own generous spirits. Other times, however, their gifts come in full recognition of the need of the recipient or because of their regard for the person to whom they are giving the gift.

Whether the favor is large or small, church ladies, like everyone else, have a perfect right to expect that it will be acknowledged in some way. Christian charity notwithstanding, common courtesy demands that when one is done a good turn, one responds in kind.

This does not mean that church ladies do good deeds with any hope of being thanked or even noticed. Far from it. More often than not, they pour themselves out in service to others without ever counting the cost.

But, oh, to see the joy reflected on their faces when the church notices their contributions! Nothing is sweeter than a church service that includes a personal thank-you from the beneficiaries of the church ladies' kindness. Whether it is a bouquet of flowers presented by a group of children or a certificate of appreciation signed by the pastor, tokens of gratitude matter to church ladies—as do more personal symbols of gratitude. Handwriting a thank-you note is one of the most thoughtful gestures anyone can ever make, and that is especially true in the church community.

You can be sure that when church ladies teach etiquette classes to young people in their congregation the art of writing thank-you notes is part of the curriculum.

"It takes five minutes to write a thank-you note, but the good feelings you generate can last forever," one church lady explained to her young charges.

"Be sure you mention the gift or the good deed in the note and say something about what it means to you. Then say thank you again, sign your name, and it's done," she went on, making short work of a social obligation many people avoid because they think it will be too much trouble.

Another, who had been a member of her congregation for more than sixty years, privately lamented the fact that her church's First Lady never bothered to say thank you to anyone for anything.

"Not for the birthday brunch we give her every year, regular as clockwork, not for the First Lady's Tea we put so much time into, not even for the Easter lilies we send to her house. She never even tells us thank you, let alone write a note."

While that lamentable lapse of good manners on the part of the First Lady certainly rankles this particular church lady, it has not yet stopped her from continuing to honor her First Lady.

Church ladies tend to keep private their complaints about such behavior. They may have a lot to say in small, select circles, but they would sooner walk over burning coals than publicly admit how put out they are by people who take their kindness for granted.

And that gracious level of discretion is what good manners are all about.

Ty Wise's Fry Bread

Fry bread or johnnycake is popular throughout the Caribbean and in some parts of the American South. Not quite a yeast roll and not quite a pancake, it can be made fast and is both filling and delicious. Ty Wise frequently makes fry bread for Family and Friends Sunday Dinner at the Norbeck Community Church.

MAKES 14 SERVINGS

1/3 cup sugar

1 cup warm water

1 or 2 cakes yeast

1 1/2 pounds white flour (3 1/3 cups flour per pound)

1 teaspoon salt

1 1/2 sticks butter, softened at room temperature

1 quart vegetable oil

In a bowl, combine the sugar and water, stir in the yeast, and let the mixture stand for a few minutes until the yeast begins to bubble. In another bowl, stir the flour to remove any lumps, then stir in the salt. Add the flour mixture to the yeast mixture and blend in the butter. Knead until you have a smooth dough. Cover and let rise until the dough has doubled in size, about 3 hours. When the dough has risen, pull off pieces the size of lemons, roll them into balls, flatten the balls with your hand or a rolling pin, and let rise again on a floured cookie sheet. Heat 3 inches of cooking oil in a heavy skillet. When the cakes have puffed to double their size, drop them into the hot oil and fry, turning once, until both sides are golden brown. Drain on brown paper and serve hot.

Note: Fry bread can be shaken in cinnamon sugar or drizzled with honey. Or use it for sausage biscuits.

—*Tyrone Wise*

New-Fangled Cornbread

The nutty sweetness of wheat germ, a health food staple, lifts old-fashioned cornbread to new heights.

MAKES 8 SERVINGS

1/2 cup butter

3 large eggs

1 1/2 cups buttermilk

1 teaspoon salt

1/3 cup sugar

3 teaspoons baking powder

1 1/2 cups stone-ground cornmeal

1/4 cup wheat germ

1/2 cup whole wheat flour

4 tablespoons melted butter

Preheat the oven to 400 degrees. Melt the 1/2 cup butter in a 9-inch cast-iron skillet. Beat the eggs, buttermilk, salt, sugar, and baking powder together in a medium bowl. Add the cornmeal, wheat germ, and flour. Pour in the 4 tablespoons of melted butter and beat well. Pour the mixture into the skillet, put the skillet in the oven, and bake for 25 to 30 minutes or until a toothpick inserted in the middle comes out clean.

—*Beverly Crandall*

Garlic Bread

Hot, buttery garlic bread goes well with pasta dishes but can also be a stand-alone treat. Don't use margarine when you make this recipe.

MAKES 8–10 SERVINGS

1 loaf Italian bread
½ cup softened butter
¼ cup minced garlic
1 tablespoon Italian seasoning
½ cup freshly grated Parmesan cheese

Preheat the oven to 400 degrees. Slice the bread in half lengthwise. Blend the softened butter, garlic, Italian seasoning, and Parmesan cheese in a small bowl. Spread the mixture over both halves of the bread. Put the two halves back together, wrap the bread in foil, and bake about 10 to 12 minutes or until the cheese and butter melt. Slice bread before serving.

—*Lauren Cooper*

Daughters of the King

JOYCE McCANNON
ATONEMENT EPISCOPAL CHURCH
WASHINGTON, D.C.

When Joyce McCannon joined Atonement Episcopal Church in 1983, her priest, Father Hunter, put her in touch with a number of church leaders, including the ones who headed up "Daughters of the King."

This group of church ladies concentrates much of its energy on religious studies. In addition, they donate their time and service to a variety of volunteer projects throughout the year. Clearly they believe that faith demands good works.

Daughters of the King contribute financially to support church missionaries. They also give money to further the education of female seminary students. They even sew and do handwork to create layettes for young mothers and their babies.

At Christmas, the Daughters of the King prepare gaily decorated goody bags containing personal hygiene products and other gifts for nursing-home residents. In order to perpetuate their legacy of good works, these church ladies have created a junior chapter of young girls. The prayers and service of the Daughters of the King constitute a rich heritage for the young women who will come after them.

Mrs. White's Big Fat Yeast Rolls

Thirty years ago, when I was a graduate student at the University of Illinois, Mrs. White, a lovely and vivacious member of the Friday Afternoon Black Elderly Tea Group, gave me her yeast roll recipe. I struggled for weeks until I'd mastered it, only to learn later that Mrs. White herself actually preferred the convenience of a boxed mix. These are so good, however, that I think they're worth the effort.

MAKES ABOUT 2½ DOZEN ROLLS

1 cup milk
2 tablespoons sugar
2 tablespoons butter
1 teaspoon salt
1 cake yeast
¼ cup warm water
1 large egg, lightly beaten
1 (5-pound) bag all-purpose flour
¼ cup melted butter

Heat but do not boil the milk, sugar, 2 tablespoons butter, and salt in a medium saucepan. Pour the mixture into a large bowl, and let cool to lukewarm. Dissolve the yeast in the ¼ cup of warm water. Add it to the milk mixture and allow it to bubble up. Add the beaten egg and stir in enough flour to make a stiff dough. Cover the bowl and let the dough rise until doubled in bulk. Turn the dough out onto a floured board and knead until smooth. Cut the dough in half. Roll and pat each half into a flat circle and brush the circles with the melted butter. Cut both circles into pie-shaped wedges, place the wedges in a well-greased pan (do not crowd the pan), and let rise again until doubled in size. While the dough is rising, preheat the oven to 400 degrees. Bake the rolls for 20 minutes or until nicely browned.

—*Mrs. White*

Corn Muffins

Muffins just seem to make people smile, especially hot muffins dripping with butter. Try these instead of your favorite cornbread recipe and see what happens.

MAKES APPROXIMATELY 21 MUFFINS

3 large eggs, lightly beaten
1½ cups buttermilk
1 cup stone-ground cornmeal
1 cup whole wheat flour
¼ cup sugar
1 teaspoon salt
1 teaspoon baking powder
1 teaspoon baking soda
½ cup creamed corn
¼ cup shredded Cheddar cheese
1 tablespoon chopped jalapeño pepper
6 tablespoons melted butter

Preheat the oven to 400 degrees. Line 2 12-cup muffin tins with muffin papers. Beat the eggs with the buttermilk in a large bowl. Add the cornmeal, flour, sugar, salt, baking powder, and baking soda. Beat well to combine. Stir in the creamed corn, cheese, and pepper. Add the melted butter and stir until all the ingredients are well combined. Pour the batter into the prepared muffin tins, filling each cup ¾ full. Bake 20 minutes or until the tops are golden brown.

—Ben Cooper

Ce

Popovers

Easy enough for children to make and as comforting as a homemade afghan, popovers are best eaten hot from the oven with your favorite jam.

MAKES 6 SERVINGS

2 large eggs, well beaten
1 cup all-purpose flour, sifted
1 tablespoon sugar
1 scant teaspoon salt
½ cup water
½ cup whole milk

Preheat the oven to 425 degrees. Grease the cups of a 6-cup muffin tin and place it in the oven. Combine the eggs, flour, sugar, and salt in a medium bowl. Whisk in the water and then the milk until the batter is smooth and bubbly.

Remove the hot muffin tin from the oven and fill the cups a little more than half full. Bake 25 to 30 minutes or until the tops pop up and the batter is brown.

—Lauren Cooper

Ce

Cheese Biscuits

The secret to making biscuits is to mix with a light hand, and that is no mean feat. Grate the cheese and have all ingredients measured out and assembled in advance so the mixing goes fast.

MAKES 12–15 BISCUITS

2 cups sifted flour
¾ teaspoon salt
3 teaspoons baking powder
6 tablespoons solid vegetable shortening, cold
1 cup grated sharp Cheddar cheese
¾ cup plus 3 tablespoons milk

Sift the flour with the salt and baking powder. Using a pastry blender, cut in the shortening, then the cheese. With a fork, stir in the milk until the ingredients are just blended and holding together. Place the dough on a sheet of floured waxed paper and roll it to about ½ inch thick. Chill for an hour. Preheat the oven to 450 degrees. Remove the dough from the refrigerator and with a floured juice glass, cut it into rounds. Place the biscuits on a well-greased baking sheet and bake 8 to 10 minutes or until lightly browned.

—*Adapted from* Secrets of Southern Maryland Cooking: How to Keep Daddy Home

℀

Fluffy Spoon Bread

Spoon bread is an old-fashioned delicacy that falls somewhere between plain cornbread and corn custard. If you've never had the pleasure of eating it with fried chicken, you've missed a real treat. My home-ec partner from high school contributed this recipe.

MAKES 8–10 SERVINGS

4 cups half-and-half
1 cup white self-rising cornmeal
5 tablespoons butter, plus additional for
    serving
1/3 cup sugar
1 1/2 teaspoons salt
4 large eggs, well beaten

Preheat the oven to 400 degrees. Grease a 9-by-9-inch baking dish. Heat the half-and-half in a double boiler until you see a ring of bub-

bles around the edge. Whisk in the cornmeal, stirring constantly. Continue stirring until the mixture reaches a pudding-like consistency. Stir in the 5 tablespoons butter, the sugar, and the salt. Add a bit of the hot mixture to the beaten eggs and whisk well. Add the warmed eggs to the hot mixture and beat well to combine. Pour mixture into the prepared baking dish and bake 35 to 45 minutes or until set. Serve the spoon bread topped with pats of additional butter.

—*Beverly Crandall*

℀

Banana Nut Bread

It almost never fails. If you must be part of a church meeting that promises to be a bit tense, bring a loaf of warm banana nut bread and most people will mind their manners.

MAKES 1 LOAF

2 cups wholewheat flour
1 teaspoon baking soda
3/4 teaspoon salt
3/4 cup peanut oil
1 cup sugar
2 large eggs
3 large, very ripe bananas, mashed
1/2 cup chopped pecans
1/4 cup apricot preserves

Preheat the oven to 325 degrees. Grease a 6-cup loaf pan. Sift the flour, baking soda, and salt together in a medium bowl. Using an electric mixer, cream the oil and sugar in a large bowl; add the eggs, beating well. Beat in the mashed bananas until the mixture is smooth. Stir in the flour mixture, nuts, and apricot preserves. Pour into the prepared loaf pan.

Bake 1 hour 25 minutes or until a toothpick inserted into the middle comes out clean.

—*Brenda Rhodes Miller*

Sift the dry ingredients together in a large bowl. Add the currants and just enough buttermilk to form a soft dough. Flour your hands and pat the dough into a ½-inch-thick circle. Cut it into wedges. Grease a griddle and heat it on medium-low to low heat. Add the scone wedges and cook 3 to 4 minutes, until lightly browned on the bottom, then turn and brown the tops for 3 to 4 minutes longer. Alternatively, you can bake the scones at 350 degrees for 15 minutes or until golden. Sprinkle with confectioners' sugar, if desired. Serve with raspberry jam.

—*Adapted from* Beard on Bread

Church Tea Scones

No self-respecting church ladies' tea could call itself complete without flaky homemade scones served with raspberry jam.

MAKES 4 SERVINGS

1 cup all-purpose flour
1 teaspoon cream of tartar
¼ teaspoon salt
2 teaspoons sugar
1 teaspoon baking soda
½ cup golden currants
½–1 cup buttermilk
Confectioners' sugar, for sprinkling,
    optional
Raspberry jam, for serving

Who Doesn't Love Hush Puppies?

Hush puppies and fried fish are meant for each other. You can make these flat or round, but please do try making them.

MAKES 6–8 SERVINGS

1 quart vegetable oil, for frying
1 cup yellow cornmeal
¾ cup all-purpose flour
1½ teaspoons baking powder
3 large eggs, well beaten
½ cup milk
¼ teaspoon salt

Heat the oil in a large skillet. Blend the dry ingredients in a medium bowl. Add the eggs and milk and stir until you have a sticky dough. Scoop up portions of batter with a tablespoon and, using a second spoon, slide it into the hot oil. Fry until golden brown. Drain on brown paper. Serve with fried seafood.

—*Adapted from* A Dash of Sevillity

CHAPTER 3

Cold Salads

Children Should Be Seen but Not Heard,
Unless It Is Time for Them to Sing in the Christmas Cantata
or Say Their Easter Speeches

THE VIEWS OF CHURCH LADIES CONCERNING HOW CHILDREN SHOULD BEHAVE AT CHURCH

"*I*n my day, children knew how to act." God alone knows how many times that statement has been uttered by church ladies who are aghast at the behavior of someone else's children. It is a comment often accompanied by a sad shake of the head, a noisy cluck of the tongue, and a look of infinite resignation that comes right before a wordless snort of disgust.

Well-meaning parents sometimes forget that the delightful antics of their children can be a source of annoyance to others. For these parents it can be a major trial just to get their children dressed and ready for Sunday service, and they may be so exhausted by their morning struggle that they fail to see how church can provide an ideal opportunity for them to teach their children valuable lessons about how to behave in public.

Historically, children have been assigned clearly defined roles in the African American church. While these roles may not have been of their choosing, they and the adults understood what was expected of them.

Sydney Cusic of New Life Christian Ministries in Chicago, Illinois,
where her father is the pastor, practicing the famous church lady look.

Generally, the role of the child is to be seen and not heard. This age-old demand of the African American church community—formulated during the cruel and painful days of segregation as an attempt to protect black children by keeping them silent in public—may now, however, be at odds with modern parenting styles that allow children to express themselves freely.

Small children are well known as world-class wiggle worms. It is just their nature to squirm and to chatter. They are easily dis-

tracted and can become cranky when tired.

The eleven o'clock morning worship service often extends into children's nap time. Yet many church ladies hold to the somewhat unrealistic belief that other folks' little children will sit quietly for several hours at a stretch just because they are in church.

Hardly anyone would disapprove of a young child's drawing or coloring quietly throughout the service. But when children thrash about and make noise during the sermon, when they whine and cry and demand attention, adult eyes start rolling and you can hear pocketbooks all over the church snapping open as church ladies dig for Peppermint Starlight Mints and other distracting goodies to offer the tiny miscreants.

And God help the hapless little boy or girl who aims repeated kicks at the pew in front of him or her. The icy glance thrown over the shoulder of the church lady seated there may not freeze the child in his tracks, but will certainly chill the blood of the child's parent and give the poor soul pause.

Parents of crying babies are strongly encouraged to go outside and walk them to sleep before returning to service. Lucky are those who attend churches with a soundproof glass family room at the back of the sanctuary. This is a wonderful innovation that allows parents to participate in the service without drawing the ire of other worshippers.

Some churches even provide nurseries for children under six. There, children can be children, watched over by dedicated attendants while their parents praise God in peace.

Older children who have learned to sit still in school may participate in Children's Church, which usually takes place during part or all of the regular morning worship service. There they learn to sing hymns at the same time they are learning to read in school, praising God in their own way. Gum chewing and loud talking out of turn are forbidden during Children's Church, but squirming is permitted.

As they worship together, children learn a principal fact of communal worship: that they must not disturb others as they praise the Lord.

While Sunday worship is the centerpiece of church life, it is only one aspect of being in communion with a congregation. Parents are encouraged to bring their children to church so they can participate in all the programs, services, and activities especially designed for children and families.

It is incumbent on parents to get the children to choir practice and rehearsals so that they will learn what to do and how to act, helping them memorize their parts for the Easter program, the Christmas pageant, and other events where speeches are part of the program.

While some intolerant church ladies suck their teeth and roll their eyes at the behavior of children not their own during the worship service, others—and they are indeed the real church ladies—are guided by the Spirit.

They square their shoulders, pick up their purses, and sit themselves right next to struggling parents to lend a much needed hand with children who are tired, cranky, and out of sorts.

It is no fun to give up the personal calm of listening to the sermon in order to help an overwhelmed parent quiet a fussy child, but by doing just that church ladies prove over and over that "it is better to light one little candle than it is to curse the darkness."

God bless them, every one.

Light and Lovely Summer Salad

If you are lucky enough to have a summertime garden, you'll love using your fresh produce in this salad. Otherwise, make friends with the vendors at your local farmer's market so that you can serve this dish.

MAKES 6–8 SERVINGS

2 large ripe tomatoes
1 large Vidalia or other sweet onion
1 large cucumber
3 tablespoons fresh basil
Salt and freshly ground pepper to taste
Bottled Italian dressing

Wash the vegetables. Core and chop the tomatoes. Peel and roughly chop the onion and cucumber. Shred the basil. Toss the vegetables and basil in a bowl. Add salt and pepper to taste, and toss with enough dressing to coat the vegetables well. Refrigerate for at least 1 hour before serving.

—Lauren Cooper

Calypso Potato Salad

If you don't like dill, feel free to substitute fresh tarragon. Most grocery stores now carry a nice assortment of fresh herbs.

MAKES 6–8 SERVINGS

1 teaspoon salt, for the cooking water
6 large white potatoes, peeled and cubed
1 cup peeled and deveined shrimp
2 tablespoons olive oil
4 tablespoons finely chopped fresh dill
1 cup unflavored yogurt
Salt and pepper to taste
Several sprigs of fresh dill, for garnish

Bring 6 quarts of water to a rolling boil; add 1 teaspoon salt and the potatoes. Cook until the potatoes are fork tender. Drain and chill them in the refrigerator for at least one hour. (Save the potato water for soup, if you wish.) Toss the shrimp in the olive oil and broil on high for 3 to 5 minutes or until the shrimp are bright pink. Coarsely chop the shrimp and chill them in the refrigerator for at least 1 hour. In a large bowl, combine the dill and yogurt; add salt and pepper to taste, and mix in the chilled potatoes and shrimp. Place in an attractive serving bowl, and garnish with springs of fresh dill. Refrigerate until ready to serve.

—Jacqueline A. Duodu

Not-So-Plain Potato Salad

MAKES 8–10 SERVINGS

½–¾ cup ranch dressing
¼ cup yellow mustard
Dash of hot sauce
⅓ cup sweet pickle relish
½ cup finely chopped red onion
3 stalks celery, finely chopped
½ cup chopped green, red, or yellow pepper
4½ cups cooked white potatoes,
    peeled and cubed
Salt and pepper to taste

Combine the ranch dressing, mustard, hot sauce, and pickle relish in a large bowl. Add the onion, celery, and pepper and mix well. Add the cooked potatoes and toss to combine. Add salt and pepper to taste and refrigerate until ready to serve.

—Lauren Cooper

Church baby Lauren Cooper attends a wedding with her grandmother Carolyn Rhodes.

Sara's Autumn Potato Salad

Small, new red potatoes are essential for this dish. Scrub them well and cook them in their skins. The apples add a nice crunch and a bit of sweetness to the salad.

MAKES 8–10 SERVINGS

12 new red potatoes, unpeeled, well washed,
    and quartered
5 slices bacon
1 cup thinly sliced onions
3 tablespoons vegetable oil
1 cup cored and chopped Granny Smith
    apples
1½ cups mayonnaise
Salt and pepper to taste

Cook the potatoes in a large saucepan, in about 6 quarts boiling salted water, until tender. Preheat the oven to 350 degrees. Place the bacon slices in a single layer on a cookie sheet, and bake until crisp. Drain on brown paper, pat with paper towels to remove all the grease, and crumble. Sauté the sliced onions in the vegetable oil until they are translucent and golden in color. Remove with a slotted spoon. Put the potatoes, apples, and onions in a large bowl, toss with the mayonnaise, and add the crumbled bacon. Taste and adjust the seasoning with salt and pepper. Refrigerate until ready to serve.

—Maria Sara Garcia

Cousin 'Nita's Potato Salad

There are as many great potato salad recipes as there are great cooks. Like recipes for gumbo, deviled eggs, macaroni and cheese, and pound cake, each potato salad recipe has just that little variation that makes it great. Every Mardi Gras, my cousin Juanita Eaton serves one of my all-time favorite potato salads.

MAKES 12–15 SERVINGS

5 pounds (about 5 or 6 large) white potatoes, peeled and boiled until tender
6 large hard-cooked eggs
1 medium onion, chopped very fine

2 stalks celery, chopped fine
½ to ¾ cup chopped sweet pickles (not relish)
1½ cups mayonnaise (or more if needed to mix well)
1 tablespoon prepared mustard
1 teaspoon sugar
Salt and pepper to taste
Paprika to taste

Cut the potatoes into small cubes. Chop the eggs. Toss together all the ingredients except the paprika, being sure to coat everything with the mayonnaise. Cover and chill overnight to meld the flavors. Sprinkle with paprika before serving.

—Juanita Eaton

Cranberry Salad

While she's often referred to as "the cake lady," Mrs. Cornell Sharperson is adept at preparing mouthwatering dishes of all kinds. She recommends serving her Cranberry Salad with her Chicken Casserole (page 88).

MAKES 6–8 SERVINGS

1 (3-ounce) package cranberry or any red gelatin
1 (14-ounce) can jellied cranberry sauce
2 cups chopped raw apples
1 cup chopped banana

Prepare the gelatin according to package directions. Stir in the cranberry sauce. Mix in the apples and bananas and refrigerate overnight or until firm.

—*Mrs. Cornell Sharperson*

Ce

Fancy Romaine Salad

The salad spinner is, in my opinion, one of the world's greatest inventions. You can whip up this salad in a flash if you use packaged croutons, although it only takes about fifteen minutes to make your own. Freshly grated Parmesan is essential; the prepackaged kind makes the salad much too salty.

MAKES 4–6 SERVINGS

2 cloves garlic
2 slices stale bread
3 tablespoons olive oil
1 (2-ounce) can anchovy fillets
1 cup bottled Caesar dressing, or less,
*   if desired*
1 large head romaine lettuce, washed and
*   spun dry*
6 large white mushrooms, wiped clean and
*   sliced*
¼ cup freshly grated Parmesan cheese

Preheat the oven to 300 degrees. Peel the garlic and rub it over both sides of the bread. Cut the bread in cubes, toss in the olive oil, and bake on a cookie sheet until the croutons are lightly toasted. Remove from the oven; rub again with the garlic and set aside. With a fork, mash the anchovy fillets with the salad dressing. Tear the lettuce into bite-sized pieces and toss it with the mushrooms in the anchovy salad dressing mixture. Sprinkle the grated Parmesan over the lettuce and top with your homemade croutons.

Note: You can substitute anchovies with no added salt for the regular anchovies, if desired.

—*Jay Cooper*

Ce

Carnival Salad

The purple, green, and gold colors of Mardi Gras are what give this salad its name. The ripe Roma tomatoes provide an extra kick of color and flavor.

MAKES 12 SERVINGS

Dash of olive oil
2 (16-ounce) bags frozen white shoepeg corn
2 (16-ounce) bags frozen baby lima beans
1 medium Bermuda (red) onion, peeled and
*   sliced thin*
2 ripe Roma tomatoes, seeded and
*   chopped*
1 to 1½ cups mayonnaise
Creole seasoning, to taste
1 head Romaine lettuce, washed and dried

Do Lord Remember Me

ANNETTA MARIA THOMAS
MT. OLIVE AME ZION CHURCH
PRICHARD, ALABAMA

When my father became too ill to care for himself, my sisters and I employed a series of home health aids to attend him. Each of the women we met brought special gifts for which we are ever grateful.

One in particular, Annetta Maria Thomas, proved to be not only an exceptionally good cook but also a real self-starter. The first task she assigned herself was to hand wash all the crystal in our late mother's china cabinet. After Annetta finished with those glasses, every single one sparkled like new, which pleased Daddy to no end.

Later she assembled his walker and shower chair. At the time, I was too overwrought to remember where Daddy kept his toolbox, so she canvassed the neighborhood, borrowing tools to complete the task.

When she was on duty, Annetta vacuumed and dusted, changed Daddy's pajamas and sheets, did his laundry, watered the plants, brought in the mail and the newspaper, made grocery lists, answered the phone, and took messages. And she did all these household chores with loving kindness and attention to detail.

Freed from such tasks, my sisters and I were able to spend our time just being with Daddy. It was a precious gift. She brought comfort to us as well as to our father. She sang while she worked, and many times she just patted Daddy's hand as she prayed for him.

No matter how reluctant Daddy might be about eating, Annetta was always able to coax him to take just one more bite.

In time, my father came to refer to his helpers as his family. At first, this was a bitter pill for his daughters to swallow. We wondered how our daddy could admit virtual strangers into the charmed circle of our family life. As they cared for him, we came to understand that family is a flexible construct.

Daddy died May 26, 2003.

After Daddy's funeral, Annetta sat with us during the repast that the Good Samaritans at church prepared. She had become family indeed.

Bring 4 quarts of salted water to a rolling boil. Add a dash of olive oil and the frozen vegetables and cook for about 10 minutes. Drain and cool the vegetables. In a large bowl, combine the cooked vegetables, the onion, and the tomatoes with the mayonnaise. Add Creole seasoning to taste and refrigerate overnight. Mix well before serving on a bed of lettuce.

—*Juanita Eaton*

Cee

Church Supper Broccoli Salad

Every family boasts a special, traditional holiday dish. This one is a salad my husband's family always serves when company comes.

MAKES 8–10 SERVINGS

1 tablespoon distilled white vinegar
¾ cup sugar
½–1 cup salad dressing (such as Miracle Whip)
1 bunch broccoli, blanched and chopped
1 cup toasted sunflower seeds
1 cup yellow raisins
1½ cups chopped green onions
6–8 slices bacon, cooked crisp and crumbled

In a small bowl, combine the vinegar, sugar, and salad dressing and mix until well blended.

In a large bowl, combine the cooked broccoli, sunflower seeds, raisins, green onions, and crumbled bacon. Pour the dressing over the broccoli mixture, mix well, and refrigerate until ready to serve.

—*Reverend Clarence Earl Miller*

Cee

Festive Cole Slaw

Even people who say they don't like cole slaw will enjoy this colorful and crisp version of an old standby. Serve it with broiled chicken or pork for a refreshing summer meal any time of the year.

MAKES 4–6 SERVINGS

1 red bell pepper
1 green bell pepper
1 yellow bell pepper
1 small red cabbage, cut in half
1 small green cabbage, cut in half
1 (8-ounce) bottle poppy seed salad dressing
Pinch of sugar
Salt and pepper to taste

Wash, seed, and julienne the bell peppers. Core the cabbage halves. Remove and discard any blemished leaves. Dip the cabbage halves in salted water and shake off the excess. Pull the leaves apart, and pat them dry. Roll up the leaves and slice them thin. This will give you shredded cabbage. Toss the shredded peppers and shredded cabbages together in a large bowl. Pour the salad dressing over the pepper and cabbage mixture and season to taste with the sugar, salt, and pepper. Refrigerate overnight, and toss again before serving.

—Joyce Ladner

Ce

Old-Fashioned Cole Slaw

What would a picnic be without a big bowl of cole slaw? You can make it sweeter by adding a bit more sugar. Add an assortment of fresh vegetables, such as chopped tomatoes, bell peppers, or radishes, for color and flavor. If you like pickled vegetables, include thinly sliced olives, chopped artichoke hearts, hot peppers, and capers to update the dish.

MAKES 8–10 SERVINGS

4 cups chopped cabbage
1 small Vidalia onion, chopped fine
1/2 cup thinly sliced celery
1/2 cup grated carrots
3/4 cup apple cider vinegar
1/2 cup sugar
1 teaspoon celery salt
1 teaspoon garlic powder
1 teaspoon dry mustard

1/2 teaspoon pepper
3/4 cup vegetable oil

Toss all the vegetables together in a large glass bowl. Heat the vinegar and next 5 ingredients on the list in a small saucepan, stirring to blend the wet and dry ingredients. Drizzle the oil into the mixture and whisk to blend. Boil for 1 minute, then remove from the heat. Cool the mixture to room temperature and pour it over the vegetables, mixing well. Cover and refrigerate overnight.

—Lolita Cusic

Ce

Vacation Bible School Macaroni and Tuna Salad

Quick and easy, this is a low-cost dish that you can dress up by using bow-tie pasta or other fancy shapes children will enjoy eating.

MAKES 8 SERVINGS

1 (16-ounce) box elbow macaroni
1 cup mayonnaise
2 tablespoons dried seafood seasoning
3 (6-ounce) cans tuna in oil
1 cup finely chopped green onions
1/2 cup chopped green onion stems,
    for garnish

Cook the macaroni according to package directions until soft but not mushy. Combine the mayonnaise and seafood seasoning in a small bowl. Drain the oil from the tuna and reserve the oil. Toss the macaroni, onions, and tuna with the mayonnaise mixture. If it is too stiff, add a bit of the reserved tuna oil. Refrigerate until ready to serve. Top with green onion stems just before serving.

—Jacqueline A. Duodu

Rice Salad

This salad is a tasty way to use up leftover rice and other bits and pieces you may have on hand. Feel free to make substitutions.

MAKES 8 SERVINGS

4 cups cooked white rice, cooled
1 cup cooked sweet peas, drained
1 cup chopped Bermuda onion
1 cup chopped ham
½ cup shredded carrots
1 (8-ounce) bottle Italian dressing or dressing
   of your choice

Mix the first 5 ingredients on the list in a large bowl. Pour the dressing over the rice mixture and combine thoroughly, being careful not to mash down the rice. Refrigerate until ready to serve. Toss again before serving.

—Beverly Crandall

Vegetable Relish

This dish uses only four ingredients, and it gets better if you keep it in the refrigerator for a day or two before serving.

MAKES 2 SERVINGS

3 large carrots, chopped
1 green bell pepper, seeded and chopped
2 stalks celery, chopped
1 cup oil and vinegar salad dressing

In a bowl, combine the chopped vegetables and toss with the salad dressing. Refrigerate until ready to serve.

—Melanie Shelwood

Better Beets

If your only acquaintance with beets is the bottled variety, this dish may turn you into a full-fledged fan.

MAKES 4–6 SERVINGS

2 cups (about 2 medium-to-large) beets,
   cooked in boiling salted water until
   tender, and cooled
½ cup maple syrup
¼ cup freshly squeezed lemon or lime juice
¼ cup orange juice with pulp

Every Day Will Be Howdy, Howdy and No Good-byes

MRS. ICIE BETTIS
PRIEST CREEK BAPTIST CHURCH
PALMERS CROSSING, MISSISSIPPI

Aunt Icie made a practice of having her young niece Joyce accompany her to just about every funeral in their neck of the woods.

She believed everyone who had cast off this mortal coil deserved to be mourned, and Aunt Icie wanted her niece to understand this, too.

Those poor unfortunates who died without friends and family to mark their passing were the ones toward whom Aunt Icie felt a special responsibility.

In those days, people wore black to funerals as a matter of course, as a way to convey respect for the deceased. The silent testimony of even a few mourners filing into the church decently garbed in black was an indication of the community's sympathy as well as its strength and resilience.

Wearing their mourning clothes and hats, Aunt Icie would take the child Joyce by the hand and sit with her on the mourner's bench. There they would cry real tears for the person who had died.

"Everybody is somebody's child," Aunt Icie would whisper to Joyce, who was immediately overcome by grief each time she heard her Aunt Icie's words. And although she was still a little girl at the time, Joyce came to understand and appreciate her aunt's personal expression of pain at the loss of a fellow human being.

What's more, because of her love for Aunt Icie, Joyce felt that she shared in the loss. She remembers being overcome by grief just as if she had actually known and loved the deceased. But she does not remember ever feeling a sense of despair.

The hope of Resurrection is what she took away from her frequent participation in the funerals of strangers, and she credits her Aunt Icie with teaching her this priceless lesson.

There is a saying in the church, "Over in Glory, every day will be howdy, howdy and no good-byes. Every day will be Sunday and Sabbath will have no end."

That joyous message was not lost on the child, and it is one that sustains Joyce Ladner to this day.

1 teaspoon salt

Dash of nutmeg

1 teaspoon minced fresh rosemary leaves

Peel and slice the beets. In a blender, combine the maple syrup, juices, salt, and nutmeg. Pulse to mix thoroughly. Pour the syrup and juice mixture over the beets, add the rosemary, and toss well. Refrigerate, tossing every few hours so the beets are coated with the liquid.

—Millicent Bolden

Ce

Tomato and Mozzarella Cheese Salad

Sweet, ripe tomatoes are the essential ingredient in this dish. Fresh basil, good-quality olive oil, and good mozzarella are summer staples.

MAKES 6–8 SERVINGS

2 very ripe, sweet tomatoes

1 pound fresh mozzarella cheese

1 cup fresh basil leaves

1 cup olive oil

1/4 cup balsamic vinegar

Slice or chop the tomatoes and mozzarella. If you use sliced tomatoes and cheese, top each tomato slice with a slice of cheese and a basil leaf. If you use chopped ingredients, combine the chopped cheese, tomatoes, and basil in a

bowl. Pour the olive oil and balsamic vinegar over the salad. Refrigerate until ready to serve.

—Brenda Rhodes Miller

Ce

Pride of Mobile West Indies Salad

Packaged crabmeat has already been cooked, which is why lump crabmeat is white rather than translucent. Serve your West Indies Salad with ripe mango and cantaloupe slices for a truly tropical delight.

MAKES 2 SERVINGS AS MAIN COURSE,
4 AS SIDE SALAD

1 medium white onion, chopped very fine

2 ice cubes

2 bay leaves

Salt and pepper to taste

1 pound cooked lump crabmeat

1/2 cup vegetable oil

1/3 cup cider vinegar

1 ripe mango

1/2 ripe cantaloupe

Flat-leaf parsley or mint leaves, for garnish

In a glass bowl, combine the onion, ice cubes, bay leaves, seasoning to taste, and the crabmeat. Toss lightly, being careful not to break up the lumps of crab.

Mix the oil and vinegar and pour the dressing over the crabmeat. Cover the bowl with plastic wrap and refrigerate 1 hour or overnight. To serve, slice and peel the fruits and arrange them on individual serving plates. Remove portions of the crabmeat from the bowl with a slotted spoon and place beside the fruit. Garnish with parsley or mint. The salad can also be served on a bed of greens.

—Melanie Shelwood

℃

Salmon Salad

Use fresh salmon fillets, grilled, baked, or poached, in this recipe. If you're really pressed for time, substitute good-quality canned salmon.

MAKES 2–3 SERVINGS

½ cup sour cream
½ cup minced onion
5 tablespoons drained capers
1 tablespoon finely chopped fresh dill weed
3 cups salmon broken into large chunks (if using canned, remove bones and skin and drain off liquid)
Salt and pepper to taste
1 head Boston lettuce, washed and dried
2 large, ripe tomatoes, cut into wedges
Fresh dill for garnish

Combine the sour cream, minced onion, capers, and chopped dill in a large bowl. Toss

with the salmon. Add salt and pepper to taste, and chill for several hours or overnight.

To serve, place a scoop of salad on a lettuce leaf, arrange the tomato wedges around the salmon, and garnish with a sprig of dill.

—Wiley L. Bolden

℃

Cooling Hot Weather Salad

Sweltering summer temperatures call for light and refreshing foods. This recipe is adapted from my grandmother's copy of *The Household Searchlight Recipe Book*.

MAKES 4 SERVINGS

1 cup diced pink grapefruit sections
1½ cups finely diced celery
¼ cup minced dates
¼ cup diced candied ginger
2 cups diced bananas
½ cup bottled poppy seed dressing
1 head Boston lettuce, washed and dried
1 cup orange sections, thin skin and membranes removed

In a glass bowl, combine the grapefruit, celery, dates, ginger, and bananas. Toss with the poppy seed dressing, and refrigerate for at least 2 hours. Arrange the lettuce leaves on 6 or 8 salad plates. Spoon the fruit salad onto the lettuce and garnish with the orange sections.

—*Adapted from* The Household Searchlight Recipe Book

Cee

Ginger Beer and Mandarin Orange Salad

The bite of ginger beer combined with the sweetness of mandarin oranges makes this salad a winner. If you can't find ginger beer, you can use good-quality ginger ale instead.

MAKES 4–6 SERVINGS

1 (3-ounce) package orange-flavored
    gelatin
2 tablespoons sugar
1 cup ginger beer
½ cup orange juice
2 cups drained canned mandarin orange
    slices

Prepare the gelatin according to package directions. Stir in the sugar and blend well. Refrigerate the gelatin mixture for about 1 hour. Add the ginger beer and orange juice and chill until the mixture is nearly set. Remove from

the refrigerator and fold in the mandarin orange slices. Chill until gelatin mixture is firm. Serve in slices or scoops.

—*Shirlene Archer*

Cee

Simple Sweet and Sour Cucumber Salad

Serve this salad as a side dish with highly seasoned foods. It should be eaten within a few hours of preparing so that the cucumbers retain some of their crunch.

MAKES 6 SERVINGS

2 large cucumbers
¼ cup sugar
¼ cup apple cider vinegar

Wash and peel cucumbers. Slice them in half lengthwise and scoop out the seeds with a spoon. Cut the cucumbers into chunks and place them in a medium bowl. Sprinkle the sugar over the cucumbers and stir. Drizzle on the vinegar and toss lightly.

—*Leslie Williams*

Cee

Trade Winds Arranged Salad

If your Women's Ministry holds its annual luncheon when avocados are plentiful, by all means volunteer to bring this salad.

MAKES 4–6 SERVINGS

1 bunch fresh spinach, washed well, stems removed, torn into bite-sized pieces
1 ripe avocado, peeled and sliced
1 (8-ounce) can hearts of palm, drained and cut into rounds
1 (4-ounce) jar marinated artichoke hearts, drained and sliced
1 medium red onion, thinly sliced
1 (16-ounce) bottle green goddess dressing

On each plate, arrange a bed of fresh spinach leaves. Over the spinach, arrange a fan of three slices of avocado, three rounds of hearts of palm, one or two slices of artichoke, and several slices of onion. Drizzle the dressing over the salad and serve immediately.

—Jacqueline A. Duodu

Vegetables

and Side Dishes

Wearing White Isn't Just for Purity—
It Can Also Stand for Sincerity

WHAT CHURCH LADIES SAY ABOUT WEDDINGS

You know you're in trouble when your future mother-in-law tells you, "I think it's just fine for you to wear white for your wedding. It isn't just for purity you know. It can also stand for sincerity."

Clearly, danger looms in your future. Especially when the soon-to-be mother-in-law is a dyed-in-the-wool Catholic church lady who attends daily Mass and weekly devotions and is, in addition, a card-carrying member of the Blue Army, a group devoted to the Blessed Virgin Mary.

But what's a girl to do? In this case, her best course of action was to smile sweetly and, without missing a beat, move on with her wedding plans. Or at least that's what a friend—who prefers to remain nameless—told me she did several years ago when faced with this implied criticism of her morals.

There's nothing like a wedding to bring out the worst in people. Fathers declare no man will ever take care of their daughter the way they do. Mothers say no woman could possible love their son as much as they do. Perhaps they're right.

There was a double wedding on June 18, 1949. Wiley L. Bolden gave away two brides that day: my mother, Carolyn Bolden, to my father, Charles Rhodes, and my Aunt Doris to Murville Douglas.

Brides and grooms see their weddings as the most important day of their lives. Both want every detail to be perfect, with every single moment preserved in both photographs and videos—as if anyone ever looked at either after the fact.

And just about everyone else involved natters on endlessly about how much the whole thing is going to cost. A wedding is nothing if not an expensive and contentious proposition.

What should be a blissfully happy occasion uniting two families can all too easily turn into a battle of wills, with the religious dimension often forgotten.

Tradition once gave the parents of the bride all the cards since they were the ones who typically paid for the wedding. The parents of the groom were allowed a set number of guests and that was pretty much that.

But these days, with blended families and divorced parents, the lines often blur. Which parents' names will appear on the wedding invitation? Whose church is deemed the family church for the wedding? Who is allowed to decide what?

If a bride has both a natural father and a stepfather, who gets to walk her down the aisle? Does tradition or personal preference rule?

And if the groom's parents have both remarried, which couple hosts the rehearsal dinner, if there is one? Where do the new spouses sit during the ceremony?

If there are blood siblings as well as stepsiblings, which ones should be invited to be wedding attendants? Most important, who on earth is objective enough to sort it all out?

Adding to the confusion is the reality that many couples now marry later in life than their own parents did. A financially independent engaged couple may decide to foot all the wedding expenses themselves. And they think, not without reason, that this ought to give them the last word on their wedding ceremony. That's when it can get sticky.

Leaving aside couples wanting a church wedding without having any real church affiliation, the increasingly complex nature of modern weddings has led some churches to establish wedding ministries with members designated as wedding consultants.

The church ladies so charged must make sure that any wedding held in their church is both decent and orderly. They have to exercise diplomacy in working with the bride, the groom, and their families to guarantee that the wedding conforms to the accepted standards of a religious ceremony.

These church ladies weigh in on wedding plans as a matter of course, but with some trepidation. As guardians of culture and tradition in their congregations, church ladies retain strong opinions about the right way to do things.

Sometimes this means they will steer a middle course, appeasing all parties and minimizing conflict while retaining the dignity of the moment. That's the good part.

All too often, however, their perspective is determined by their relationship to either the families or the couple. This may lead them to ignore custom, church protocol, and the rules of etiquette, depending on who is getting married.

Say the bride selects popular rather than sacred music for her wedding ceremony. Absent clear-cut church-established guidelines, the church lady/wedding consultant may either approve or dismiss the wishes of the bride, depending on how she thinks the parents feel about the subject. Or how she feels herself.

What if a couple envisions a wedding that is a cross between the Greatest Show on Earth and a fairy tale? It is incumbent upon the wedding consultant to bring the couple back to reality, reminding them that a church wedding is a religious service first and foremost. The consultant must do this gently but firmly.

Sometimes she will and sometimes she won't. It just depends. That's the bad part. And God help the church lady who makes the wrong choice for her congregation.

What church ladies have said is that all too many brides see their weddings as a day to live out their fantasies and can completely miss the point that a wedding is when two people stand up before God and man to proclaim their mutual love and lifelong commitment.

One church lady reported on the time she was working on a wedding and thought every detail was under control and in accord with the customs of her congregation. Until she saw what the bridesmaids were wearing.

"My heart just about stopped beating when I saw their dresses. It wasn't that the brides-maids were wearing these tiny little slips that were short and strapless and gold, with feath-ers all around the hems no less. That was bad enough. But their dresses were cut down to here and split up to there. And some of the bridesmaids had visible tattoos! They looked like something out of a bad movie about cho-rus girls. But it was too late then for me to do anything about it. I learned my lesson. Now I ask the bride to show me pictures of what everyone in the wedding will be wearing be-fore I give my approval."

As long as there are weddings, there will be church ladies who either dab at their eyes with lace hankies during the ceremony or cover their faces in dismay at the way the ser-vice unfolds. That's just the way it is.

Mediterranean Spinach

In the old days, green vegetables were cooked to within an inch of their lives, sacrificing flavor and color. But there's no need to torture spinach that way. In just a few minutes you can prepare a dish that is delicious, nutritious . . . and gor-geous to boot.

MAKES 10 SERVINGS

½ cup olive oil
4 cloves garlic, peeled, sliced, and mashed
3 pounds fresh spinach, washed and stemmed
1 cup peeled, cubed ripe tomatoes
Juice of 1 lemon
Salt and pepper to taste

Heat a heavy cast-iron skillet and add the olive oil and garlic. When you can smell the garlic, add the spinach and cover the skillet. Shake the skillet until the olive oil, garlic, and spinach are well mixed, about 5 minutes. Re-move the pan from the heat, add the toma-toes, and shake again to blend. Sprinkle with the lemon juice and season with salt and pep-per just before serving.

—*Courtenay L. Miller*

Ring of Spinach

Nothing mimics the color of spring quite so emphatically as a bright green ring of spinach. This is a very versatile dish that can be used for dinner or brunch.

MAKES 4–6 SERVINGS

2 cups cooked, well-drained spinach
¼ cup chopped celery
¼ cup chopped green onion
1 clove garlic, chopped
1 tablespoon butter or margarine
1 cup soft bread crumbs
1 large lightly beaten egg
½–1 teaspoon salt
½ teaspoon pepper
½ cup shredded Cheddar cheese

Preheat the oven to 375 degrees. Grease a 12-cup ring mold with a large center opening. Chop the cooked spinach and place it in a medium bowl. In a small skillet, sauté the celery, green onion, and garlic in the butter until tender. Add to the spinach along with the bread crumbs, egg, salt, pepper, and cheese, and mix well. Pour the spinach mixture into the prepared mold and bake 20 to 25 minutes or until set. Unmold the spinach onto a platter. Fill the center with steamed rice for dinner or scrambled eggs for brunch.

—Beverly Crandall

Callaloo

Dasheen is a root vegetable whose stalks are normally used in callaloo. Dasheen bush (as the stalks are called) is available in the United States in West Indian markets, but its preparation is time-consuming and labor-intensive. The dasheen stalks must be stripped and cleaned thoroughly and the scratchy ends of the leaves must be removed. Because of the complications involved in preparing callaloo with dasheen, spinach has become a popular substitute.

MAKES 4–6 SERVINGS

1 teaspoon vegetable oil
1 small yellow onion, chopped
3 cloves garlic, minced
1 (10-ounce) box frozen chopped spinach
¼ small Spanish pumpkin, diced
½ (10-ounce) box frozen okra
1 cup coconut milk
1 teaspoon seasoned salt
½ teaspoon cayenne pepper (optional)

Heat the oil in a medium saucepan, add the onion and garlic, and simmer for 1 minute. Add the frozen spinach, pumpkin, and okra, and simmer, covered, over low heat until the pumpkin is tender. When the vegetables are almost dissolved, add the coconut milk, seasoned salt, and cayenne pepper, if desired. Cook 10 to 15 minutes longer. Serve with rice and fish.

—Shirlene Archer

Spare the Rod and Spoil the Child

PROGRESSIVE MISSIONARY BAPTIST CHURCH
EL CAMPO, TEXAS

*E*ven adult children remain subject to their parents. The commandment to "honor thy father and thy mother" does not come with a statute of limitations.

My husband recently heard the perfect example of this point. When he was in El Campo, Texas, for his great-aunt Jennie B.'s ninety-eighth birthday, relatives started talking about the old days.

Lee Edward was a full-grown man who always said, "I don't go to church because there's no sense in me lying."

But many years ago his mother insisted he accompany her to a funeral. Seeing no way out, Lee Edward complied and sat right next to his mother, Mrs. India Polk. The funeral ran long, as Baptist Home Going Celebrations tend to do.

Lee Edward leaned over and whispered to his mother that he needed to step outside for a moment to smoke a cigarette. Mrs. Polk told him to wait. But as time went on and the funeral showed no sign of coming to an end, demon tobacco had Lee Edward in its grip. Again, he told his mother he had to go smoke. And again, she told him to wait.

He fidgeted. He jiggled his leg. He tapped his foot. Finally, he lit his cigarette. When the smell of the sulfur match hit his mother's nostrils she didn't say a word. Her powerful back-hand knocked Lee Edward over along with three wooden pews behind him.

And there was Lee Edward looking up at the ceiling with his cigarette in his mouth.

Lord, have mercy.

Church ladies Mary Polk and India Polk taking a well-deserved moment of rest following a church "homecoming on the grounds" in El Campo, Texas. Both were renowned for their culinary skills and gift of hospitality.

Baked Vidalia Onions

While just about every onion will become sweet if it's cooked long enough, Vidalia onions from Georgia, however, have a head start because they're already sweet in their raw state. You can use any onions for this recipe, but only Vidalias will give you a truly sweet finish.

MAKES 4–6 SERVINGS

8 cups chopped Vidalia onions
6 tablespoons butter
1 cup raw converted rice, cooked according
    to package directions
1 cup shredded pepper jack cheese
¾ cup heavy cream

Preheat the oven to 350 degrees. Grease a 9-by-9-inch baking dish. Sauté the onions in a large skillet in 5 tablespoons of the butter until golden. Combine the cooked rice, sautéed onions, cheese, and cream in a medium bowl; mix well. Spoon the mixture into the prepared baking dish and bake for about 1 hour or until brown on top.

—Millicent Bolden

Kale or Collard Greens

For many years I foolishly viewed beautiful, curly, dark green kale as nothing more than a decorative lining for the platter upon which I served roasted turkey or baked ham at holidays. When I noticed that the vegetable was covered with delicious juices from the meat, on went the light in my head. So instead of tossing out the greens, I tossed them into the slow cooker. What a find!

If you haven't used greens as a garnish, try this recipe with fresh kale or collard greens or a mixture of both. They cook down to make a nutritious and warming side dish.

MAKES 4 SERVINGS

2 pounds fresh curly kale or fresh collard
    greens, well washed, stems removed, leaves
    left whole
1 tablespoon salt or baking soda
2 bouillon cubes, any flavor
2 cups hot water
1 cup chicken, turkey, pork, beef, or ham
    scraps

Swish the washed and trimmed greens in cold water; add the salt or baking soda, and rinse well. Dissolve the bouillon cubes in 2 cups of hot water. Stuff the greens into a slow cooker, and pour the bouillon water over them. Add more water to cover if necessary. Add the meat scraps and stir so the water is well incorporated. Cook on low for about 2 hours, stirring and adding more water as needed. Chop the greens before serving.

—Brenda Rhodes Miller

The Marriage of Turnip and Mustard Greens

Sometimes, like finding a good mate, you are lucky enough to find turnip greens with the turnips still attached. If you can't, buy a pound of fresh white and purple turnips and 2 pounds each of fresh turnip and mustard greens. The mixed greens and turnips complement each other in a way we can only pray for in the best of marriages.

MAKES 8–10 SERVINGS

2 pounds fresh or unthawed frozen turnip
    greens
2 pounds fresh or unthawed frozen mustard
    greens
½ teaspoon salt, plus additional to taste
¼ teaspoon pepper, plus additional to taste
¼ teaspoon sugar
1 pound fresh turnips, peeled and cut into
    chunks
5 tablespoons oil
1 teaspoon hot sauce, or to taste

If using fresh greens, wash them in several changes of cold, salted water to remove dirt. Pick through greens, discarding blemished or wilted greens and removing the stems. Tear greens into pieces. Mix the ½ teaspoon salt, ¼ teaspoon pepper, and the sugar in a small bowl. Toss the turnip chunks in the seasoning mixture. Heat the oil in a Dutch oven and sauté the seasoned turnip chunks until very lightly browned. Add the greens and stir to combine. Add enough water to cover greens and cook, covered, for 30 minutes. Add the hot sauce and cook for 10 minutes more. Before serving, taste and adjust seasoning with additional salt and pepper.

—Joyce Ladner

Holiday Squash Sauté

Select firm green and yellow squash and an unblemished red bell pepper for this simple dish.

MAKES 4–6 SERVINGS

1 cup chopped onion
1 clove garlic, finely minced
7 tablespoons butter
3 small yellow squash, sliced about ½ inch
    thick
3 small green squash, sliced about ½ inch
    thick
1 small red bell pepper, seeded and sliced
    thin
¼ cup cooked crumbled bacon

Sauté the chopped onion and garlic in 4 tablespoons of the butter until vegetables are tender and golden. Add the sliced squash and bell pepper and the remaining 3 tablespoons of butter. Simmer on low until tender. Stir in the crumbled bacon just before serving.

—Lolita Cusic

Everything Is Not for Everybody

RUBY SAUNDERS
BETHLEHEM BAPTIST CHURCH
GUM SPRINGS, VIRGINIA

When Ruby Saunders was a very little girl, going to church was a major source of entertainment for her. She would sit up front, secretly nibbling her cookies. She watched in amazement at the preacher jumping up and down, the choir members singing until they dropped, and people getting the Holy Ghost; she honestly thought they were doing it just for her.

She remembers an older cousin who fainted every time there was a holiday service, and she speculates that this happened because her cousin was so dressed up. Beneath her fancy clothes she wore a full complement of unaccustomed foundation garments that squeezed her every which a way.

Ruby was a young teenager when she and about fourteen of her cousins were to be baptized on the same day. Their church had a new indoor baptismal pool that had never been used. Big for her age, Ruby was an athlete and skillful swimmer. When the minister said, "I baptize you in the name of the Father, Son, and the Holy Ghost," he grabbed hold of her and tried to duck her under the water.

Ruby, however, grabbed him right back, and they both almost fell. Not to be daunted, the minister tried again. "In the name of the Father . . ." Ruby almost flipped him this time.

He tried it once more and was saved from going under only by the fact that the pool was too small to accommodate two dunkings at once.

By this time they were both soaking wet. Ruby Saunders never did get baptized, but she stayed in the church. Any wonder that her minister didn't try to baptize her again?

Jesus on the Main Line

LOLITA CUSIC
NEW LIFE CHRISTIAN MINISTRIES OF GREATER CHICAGO
CHICAGO, ILLINOIS

The lyrics of the beloved hymn "Jesus on the Main Line" came to Lolita Cusic's mind as she sat listening attentively to a visiting preacher during a recent revival.

"It was a wonderful revival and the congregation was really engaged in the sermon," Mrs. Cusic, First Lady of her church, reports.

The guest preacher was giving it his all, eloquent and full of energy as he shared a message based on Mark 5. Halfway through his sermon the unmistakable sound of a cell phone shattered the Spirit-filled atmosphere of the church. Heads turned and people looked aghast at the interruption.

But did the cell phone's owner meekly silence the offending instrument with the flip of the ringer switch? Was the blasted device simply turned off in recognition of the sacred preaching moment? Quite the contrary.

According to Mrs. Cusic, "The woman answered the phone and proceeded to carry on a lengthy conversation right there in the middle of the service! I was never so shocked in my life."

Cell phones, two-way pagers, and other means of electronic communication can be a boon to busy people on the go. But when those busy people enter church, common courtesy, not to mention plain old mother wit, should prevail.

Let's hope churches will not be forced to follow the lead of theaters. What a shame it would be to see notices in the bulletin advising churchgoers to avoid disturbing fellow worshippers with their phones and pagers. If good sense prevails congregants will put their communication devices on vibrate or just turn them off until the service ends.

After all, while the old hymn advises us to call "Jesus on the main line. . . . Call Him up, call Him up, tell Him what you want," God still manages to speak to us without resorting to the telephone.

Mama's Mashed Rutabagas with Lemon

The poor old rutabaga encased in its hard, waxy coating is the ugly stepchild among other less daunting root vegetables. But when treated nicely, as in this recipe, rutabaga makes for a lovely, golden, and flavorful change from mashed potatoes.

MAKES 4–6 SERVINGS

2 pounds whole rutabagas
1 teaspoon salt
Pinch of sugar
Juice of ½ a fresh lemon
3 tablespoons melted butter
Salt and pepper to taste

Peel the rutabagas with care using a sharp vegetable peeler. The hard, waxy coating can be tricky to remove. Chop the rutabagas into large chunks, place them in a medium saucepan, cover with water, add 1 teaspoon salt, and boil until tender. In a large bowl, with a potato masher or a large fork, mash the cooked rutabagas with a pinch of sugar and the lemon juice. Add the melted butter and beat until the mixture has the consistency of mashed potatoes. Season with salt and pepper to taste.

—Carolyn Lolita Bolden Rhodes

Nanny Med's Glazed Carrots

My sister says to use either frozen carrots or the little fresh ones sold in the produce section. Don't use canned carrots because they turn into mush.

MAKES 3–4 SERVINGS

1 pound fresh or frozen baby carrots
2 tablespoons butter
⅛ teaspoon ground ginger
¼ teaspoon cinnamon
Honey to taste

Cook the carrots in boiling water to cover until tender. Add the butter, ginger, cinnamon, and honey. (Use more or less honey depending on the sweetness you desire.) Continue cooking until the liquid is reduced to a sauce. Serve as a side dish with chicken or ham.

—Melanie Shelwood

Smooth and Easy Turnips

You can dress up even the lowly turnip with the addition of enough butter and cream. Use white turnips or rutabagas for this recipe, depending on what you like or what is available in the grocery store.

MAKES 3–4 SERVINGS

God Is Our Refuge and Our Strength

MRS. MARTHA CHUBB
MONTVALE FIRST BAPTIST CHURCH
MONTVALE, VIRGINIA

While I was writing this book, a dearly loved relative who lived with my family for more than twenty years was stricken with cancer. My husband and children and I were devastated by her sudden and unexpected death.

The experience left me both physically and emotionally exhausted, as well as spiritually bereft. Then one day, shortly after her funeral, when I was at home struggling with my grief, the telephone rang.

Mrs. Martha Chubb was on the line. I had been drawn to her when I met her at a women's retreat my church had hosted several months earlier and her presentation on the subject of prayer spoke to my heart.

As a pastor's wife, I tend to keep mum about my own troubles because people look to me for comfort and solace and strength. The day Mrs. Chubb called, however, I was at such a low ebb that I abandoned my usual reserve and cried on her telephone shoulder, telling her about my loss and how sad I was feeling.

She immediately understood and began to talk to me about her own struggles. "There was a time when I would tell my husband, you just drop me off at the corner and you go on home. I'll walk because I just need to get some peace."

Clearly, this was a woman who could understand my pain. She had searched the Scriptures for help, and when she found Psalm 46, she knew it was for her. Of all the Scriptures she had read, only this one had a female pronoun. "God is our refuge and our strength, a very present help in trouble," it begins, but it was the fifth verse that spoke specifically to her: "God is in the midst of her; she shall not be moved: God shall help her and that right early."

Her seventeen-year-old daughter, she said, had gone into intensive care the day after Christmas and stayed there two days short of a month. "God used my child to lead me to Salvation," she told me.

"The doctors said she was sitting on a powder keg and could go off at any minute. They said there was nothing they could do.

"But I read in the Upper Room that God can heal anything that man says is impossible. So I read that verse to my daughter Adrian and I saw a miracle right then. The Lord blessed her and raised her up. She was seventeen then and she's forty-seven now. She's a missionary who has been to Africa, Spain, and Haiti."

Mrs. Chubb and her husband became church planters—those who help other churches get started. They planted two churches in their own home and then went on to plant others in New Jersey and North Carolina before God brought them to Virginia where the couple was called to pastor a church.

"I'm just a little spoke, but if I can help the wheel to turn, then I'm happy. All I ask is for God to give me His holy boldness."

8 *small young turnips or rutabagas*
3 *tablespoons butter or margarine*
¼ cup heavy cream
2 *teaspoons sugar*
Salt and pepper to taste

Peel the turnips or rutabagas. Place them in a medium saucepan, cover with water, and boil until tender. Drain well. Transfer the vegetables to the container of a food processor, add 2 tablespoons of the butter, and puree until smooth. Pour in the cream, sugar, and salt and pepper. Puree until fluffy. Spoon into a warmed serving dish and top with the remaining tablespoon of butter.

—*Joyce Clemons*

Green and White Fritters

This is a great side dish to accompany fried fish.

MAKES 4–6 SERVINGS

1 *cup all-purpose flour*
3 *teaspoons baking powder*
¼ teaspoon salt
1 *cup milk*
2 *large eggs, beaten*
1 *teaspoon freshly squeezed lemon juice*
2 *cups crisply cooked cauliflower and*
    broccoli flowerets
Vegetable oil for frying

Combine the flour, baking powder, and salt in a medium bowl, mixing well. Add the milk, eggs, and lemon juice, and stir just until blended. Gently stir in the vegetables, coating them well. Heat the vegetable oil in a deep fryer or a large skillet. Drop the vegetables into the hot oil and turn until the coating is cooked on all sides. Drain on paper towels before serving.

—*Dora Finley*

℃

Winter Vegetable Medley

Even in the depths of winter you can still serve interesting and delicious vegetable dishes. Use a combination of fresh and frozen vegetables to garner the maximum vitamins and color.

MAKES 8–10 SERVINGS

1/2 pound fresh carrots
1 pound fresh or frozen broccoli flowerets
1 pound fresh or frozen cauliflower flowerets
1 whole red bell pepper
2 cups canned vegetable broth
Dash of garlic powder
Dash of black pepper

Preheat the oven to 375 degrees. Scrape and slice the fresh carrots into ¼- to ½-inch-thick rounds. Break up the broccoli and cauliflower flowerets into pieces. Seed and slice red bell pepper into strips. Combine the vegetable broth with the garlic powder and pepper in a

rectangular baking dish. Add the vegetables. Cover with foil and bake for 20 minutes.

—*Edythe Crump*

℃

Stewed Cabbage with Potatoes

If comfort food is what you're after, this is the dish for you. Cabbage is sweet and filling when it isn't overcooked. Serve it as a side dish with pork chops.

MAKES 4–6 SERVINGS

1 large head cabbage
2 large potatoes, peeled and cut in large chunks
1 teaspoon salt
3 teaspoons dried summer savory

Cut the cabbage into quarters and plunge it into a bowl of salted water. Bring 5 quarts of water to a boil in a Dutch oven. Add the cabbage, potatoes, salt, and 2 teaspoons of the summer savory, and cook until the potatoes are tender. Drain, toss with the remaining tablespoon of summer savory, and serve.

Note: If summer savory is not available, use a mixture of 1 tablespoon chopped fresh mint and 1 tablespoon chopped fresh thyme.

—*Brenda Rhodes Miller*

Asparagus in White Sauce

Fans of asparagus are always looking for one more way to serve this succulent harbinger of spring. Richer than many dishes featuring asparagus, this is still a light and lovely way to enjoy the green stalks.

MAKES 4–6 SERVINGS

1 bunch fresh asparagus
2 large hardboiled eggs, sliced
1½ cups White Sauce (recipe follows)

Preheat the oven to 350 degrees. Grease a 9-by-9-inch baking dish. Clean the asparagus, removing the tough ends. Place alternating layers of asparagus, eggs, and cream sauce in the prepared baking dish and bake 20 minutes or until browned.

White Sauce

1½ tablespoons butter
1½ tablespoons all-purpose flour
Salt and pepper to taste
1½ cups hot milk
½ cup grated cheese of your choice

Melt the butter in a medium saucepan, and add the flour and seasonings, stirring until the mixture is thickened and well blended. Add the milk gradually, stirring constantly. Bring to a boil, and boil 2 minutes. Stir in the cheese before adding the sauce to the casserole.

—Brenda Rhodes Miller

Baked Portobellos

Many churches encourage abstaining from meat during Holy Week. The robust flavor of portobello mushrooms is enough to convince even the most dedicated carnivore that being a vegetarian might not be so bad after all.

MAKES 6 SERVINGS

6 large or 12 medium fresh portobello
   mushrooms, cleaned, stems removed
2 tablespoons melted butter
Salt and pepper to taste
½ cup fine bread crumbs
¼ cup grated Parmesan cheese

Preheat the oven to 400 degrees. Grease a 9-by-12-inch baking dish. Lay the mushrooms in the prepared baking dish and brush them with the melted butter. Add salt and pepper to taste, sprinkle with the bread crumbs and the cheese, and bake 5 to 10 minutes or until the mushrooms are tender and the topping is browned.

—Courtenay L. Miller

Old-Fashioned Corn Pudding

If your Thanksgiving dinner doesn't already include corn pudding, why not give this easy recipe a try? My son has been making this dish since he was about seven years old. Canned corn is easy to find throughout the year, and corn pudding makes for a great side dish anytime you have poultry on the menu.

MAKES 16–20 SERVINGS

6 large eggs
2 cups half-and-half
1 cup sugar
4 (15-ounce) cans cream-style corn
½ cup flour
2 (15-ounce) cans plain corn
½ cup butter, melted
1 teaspoon salt
1 teaspoon pepper

Preheat the oven to 350 degrees. Lightly grease a 9-by-15-inch glass baking dish.

Beat the eggs, half-and-half, and sugar in a large bowl. Stir in the cream-style corn and the flour. Drain the canned corn and add to the mixture along with the melted butter, salt, and pepper; mix well. Pour into the prepared baking dish and bake for 60 to 75 minutes or until set. Let stand 5 to 10 minutes before serving.

—Jay Cooper

Savory Corn Pudding

Preparing Thanksgiving dinner has always been a family affair at our house. While one son concentrated on making a sweet corn pudding using an old family recipe, the other tried his hand at improvisation, combining corn and cheese with some of the vegetables used in making stuffing. Their older sister kept them on task.

SERVES 16–20

½ cup butter
2 (15-ounce) cans cream-style corn
4 (15-ounce) cans plain corn, drained
1 cup heavy cream
1 cup shredded Cheddar cheese
1 cup diced bell pepper
1 cup diced onion
1 cup diced celery
1 cup chicken broth
6 large eggs, well beaten
½ teaspoon salt
½ teaspoon pepper
1½ cups seasoned bread crumbs

Preheat the oven to 350 degrees. Melt the butter in a 4-quart glass baking dish. Mix the cream-style corn and the next 10 ingredients on the list in a large bowl; add half the bread crumbs. Mix well and transfer to the baking dish. Top with the remaining bread crumbs and bake for 1 hour or until set. Serve with poultry.

—Ben Cooper

Fried Corn

Cook sweet summer corn this way for a rich and satisfying dish.

MAKES 4–6 SERVINGS

5 ears fresh corn, shucked
Salt and pepper to taste
¾ cup half-and-half
½ cup butter
2 tablespoons all-purpose flour

Slice the corn from the cob with a sharp knife. In a medium bowl, combine the corn with the salt, pepper, and half-and-half. Melt the butter in a large skillet. Add the flour, stirring constantly until well mixed with the butter. Add the corn mixture and cook on low heat for 10 to 12 minutes, stirring constantly.

—Melanie Shelwood

Cᴇ

Hot Pepper and Corn Sauté

This recipe serves 4, but it's easy to increase. Just add more corn, peppers, and a bit more oil, depending on how many servings you want.

SERVES 4

1 ear corn
1 tablespoon olive oil
½ cup chopped red and yellow bell pepper
1 jalapeño pepper, seeded and diced
¼ cup chopped green onion
Salt and pepper to taste
1 tablespoon chopped fresh cilantro

Cut the corn from the cob. Heat the olive oil in a small sauté pan. Add the corn, bell pepper, jalapeño, and green onion. Season with salt and pepper to taste and cook until tender. Toss with the cilantro just before serving.

—Carol Martin

Cᴇ

String Bean and Mushroom Casserole

A variation of this dish was very popular in the 1950s. If you have vegetarians in your congregation, use only cream of vegetable soups and be sure to let them know they can safely eat this casserole because it does not include any meat.

SERVES 8–10

3 cups cooked canned mushrooms
3 (10½-ounce) cans cream soup, use any
    combination of cream of celery,
    mushroom, or chicken
6 cups canned string beans
1 cup French-fried onions or slivered almonds

Preheat the oven to 350 degrees. Cover the bottom of a 3-quart baking dish with the mushrooms. Combine the cream soups and stir in 1 cup water. Pour half the soup mixture over the mushrooms and spread to cover. Add the string beans and cover with the remaining soup mixture. Top with onions or almonds, cover the dish with aluminum foil, and bake 30 minutes or until the mixture bubbles and the vegetables are heated throughout.

—Brenda Rhodes Miller

Cee

Miss Rena's Special Baked Beans

Simple and easy to prepare, these baked beans taste special thanks to the brown sugar, nutmeg, and bacon.

MAKES 4–6 SERVINGS

1 (32-ounce) can baked beans (I use Bush's
 original)
½ pound thick, sugar-cured bacon
1 tablespoon brown sugar
1 teaspoon nutmeg

Preheat the oven to 350 degrees. Pour the baked beans into a 9-by-9-inch baking pan. Set aside four slices of bacon and chop the rest into bite-sized chunks. Mix the brown sugar and the nutmeg in a small bowl and stir

into the beans until well blended. Add the chopped bacon. Lay the four slices of bacon across the top of the beans and bake 30 minutes or until the bacon on top is cooked. Discard the bacon topping and serve the beans with barbecued chicken or beef.

—Rena Simmons

Ms. Rena Simmons, a woman of faith, in her sister's kitchen in 1973. It was the day Ms. Simmons returned home after completing basic training in the 220 Military Police Brigade of the United States Army in Fort McClellan, Alabama. She remembers being ready to enjoy her first home-cooked meal in quite some time.

World's Best Black-Eyed Peas

Along with collard greens, black-eyed peas are traditionally served on New Year's Day to bring good luck. The legend is that anyone who eats the peas will have plenty of coin to spend in the year to come.

MAKES 6–8 SERVINGS

1 (16-ounce) package dried black-eyed peas
1 medium onion, studded with 8 to 10
    whole cloves
4 cloves garlic, minced
1 cup chopped red bell pepper
1 teaspoon red pepper flakes
¼ pound country ham, chopped
4 (10½-ounce) cans chicken broth
¼–½ cup water, if needed toward end of
    cooking time

Rinse the black-eyed peas in a colander. Remove any bits of debris and peas that float to the top. Place the peas, clove-studded onion, garlic, bell pepper, pepper flakes, and ham in a slow cooker. Cover with the chicken broth and cook, stirring every hour, until the peas are done and the liquid is creamy. If the liquid becomes too thick, add enough water to thin it to the consistency you desire. Remove the whole cloves and serve over fluffy white rice, if desired.

—Mrs. Beulah Hughes

Green Tomato Egg Bake

If you thought green tomatoes were only good for frying, think again. This dish can be served with a salad for a lovely brunch or as a side dish to make a meal more exciting.

MAKES 4 SERVINGS

2 tablespoons butter or margarine
1 teaspoon olive oil
1½ cups chopped sweet onion
1½–2 cups chopped green tomatoes
8 large eggs
2 tablespoons grated Parmesan cheese,
    plus additional for sprinkling
½ teaspoon crushed oregano
¼ teaspoon chopped basil
Salt and pepper to taste

Heat the butter and oil in a large skillet. Add the onion and sauté until tender. Add the tomatoes and cook 5 minutes or until tender. In a medium bowl, combine the eggs, 2 tablespoons of cheese, the oregano, basil, and salt and pepper to taste. Whisk until well mixed and pour into the skillet. Lift the edges to let the uncooked egg run underneath. When almost set, remove from the heat and sprinkle with additional Parmesan cheese. Place under the broiler to set and lightly brown the eggs. Cut in wedges to serve.

—Ellen Robinson

Company Rice

For a restaurant-worthy presentation, fill small ramekins or dessert cups with this colorful and well-flavored side dish. Put a dinner plate face down over each individual ramekin or dessert cup, hold the two together, flip the plate over, remove the ramekin, and voila!—rice that is fancy enough for company. It looks very impressive surrounded by a bright green salad and grilled chicken or scallops.

MAKES 4–6 SERVINGS

1 ½ cups water
1 tablespoon olive oil
1 (5-ounce) package saffron yellow long-grain
    rice
1 cup frozen peas and carrots
1 red bell pepper, chopped fine

Bring the water and the olive oil to a boil in a medium saucepan. Add the rice and vegetables and stir well. Reduce the heat, cover, and cook 15 to 20 minutes or until the water is absorbed and the rice is tender. Fluff the rice before making decorative mounds.

—Beverly Crandall

Orange-Flavored Rice

Whether you're serving duck, chicken, or turkey, orange-flavored rice will add a sophisticated note to your meal.

MAKES 2–3 SERVINGS

1 cup uncooked rice
½ cup orange juice
1 tablespoon grated orange peel

In a medium saucepan, cook the rice according to package directions. When the rice is dry and tender, add the orange juice and orange peel and stir to combine. Cover and keep warm until the juice is absorbed.

    Note: Add chopped pecans for additional color and crunchiness.

—Dora Finley

Trinidad and Tobago Peas and Rice

Wear disposable rubber gloves to chop the peppers and be sure to throw the gloves away when you're done. The oil in these potent peppers can burn you if you accidentally touch your face with fingers that have come contact with the peppers.

This dish is extremely hot. Less adventuresome souls can substitute jalapeño peppers for the scotch bonnets.

MAKES 8–10 SERVINGS

2 tablespoons canola oil

3 tablespoons sugar

2 (15½-ounce) cans pigeon peas, drained

5 green onions, chopped

1 yellow onion, chopped fine

2 cubes chicken bouillon

3 cloves garlic, chopped

¾ to 1 cup green seasoning (available at
    Hispanic or Caribbean markets)

2 tablespoons crushed red pepper

2 scotch bonnet peppers, seeded and
    chopped

Adobo seasoning, to taste (available at
    Hispanic or Caribbean markets)

1 (14-ounce) can coconut milk

3 cups converted rice

Heat the oil in a large cast-iron pot, add the sugar, and stir until the sugar is dark brown. (Do not let it turn black because it will make the peas bitter.) Pour the peas into the pot along with all the remaining ingredients except the coconut milk and rice. Stir well. Add the coconut milk, stir, and cook on low heat until the peas break open. Add the rice and 3 cups of water. Cover and cook on low until the rice is tender. Fluff with a fork and serve.

—Shirlene Archer

Kiss-Me-Not Mashed Potatoes

Garlic is what gives these mashed potatoes an extra kick. You can leave it out, but why would anyone want to do a thing like that?

MAKES 4 SERVINGS

4 large white potatoes

6 cloves garlic, peeled

1 (3-ounce) package cream cheese

¼ cup half-and-half (or more if desired for a
    creamier texture)

Salt, pepper, and hot sauce to taste

Wash and quarter the potatoes. Leave the skins on for extra flavor. Bring 5 quarts of water to a rolling boil and add the potatoes and the garlic. Cook the potatoes until they break apart when tested with a fork. Drain in a colander set over the hot pot, so all the water is out of the cooked potatoes and garlic. Drain the pot. Return the potatoes and garlic to the pot and add the cream cheese. Mash with a potato masher. Add the half-and-half and continue mashing. Leave a few lumps so everyone will know that your mashed potatoes are homemade! Season to taste with salt, pepper, and hot sauce.

—Brenda Rhodes Miller

Super Cheesy Scalloped Potatoes

What could be more comforting than cheese and potatoes baked to a soft and creamy turn? Serve this side dish with roasted, baked, or fried chicken for a satisfying dinner.

MAKES 4–6 SERVINGS

6 medium potatoes, peeled and sliced thin
2 tablespoons all-purpose flour
½ teaspoon salt
½ teaspoon pepper
2 tablespoons butter, cut into small pieces
1½ cups milk, scalded
1½ cups shredded sharp Cheddar cheese

Preheat the oven to 350 degrees. Grease a 4-by-6-inch baking dish. Layer the sliced potatoes in the prepared baking dish. Sprinkle with the flour, salt, and pepper. Dot with the butter and pour in the milk. Top with the cheese and bake 30 minutes or until the potatoes are tender and the top is crispy and golden.

—Lolita Cusic

Savory Shredded Sweet Potatoes

While candied yams and baked sweet potatoes will always be holiday staples, you can also use the abundant autumn sweet potatoes to make another tasty side dish.

MAKES 8–12 SERVINGS

5 large raw sweet potatoes, grated
2 cups diced green bell peppers
2 cups diced onions
1 cup thinly sliced celery
1 tablespoon minced fresh sage
1 tablespoon minced fresh thyme
1½ teaspoons salt
1 teaspoon pepper
3 large eggs, beaten
1 (10¾-ounce) can chicken broth
½ cup seasoned bread crumbs

Preheat the oven to 350 degrees. Butter a 9-inch baking dish. Combine all the ingredients except the bread crumbs in a large bowl. Pour into the prepared baking dish, top with the bread crumbs, and bake 30 minutes or until set. Serve with poultry or ham.

—Jacqueline A. Duodu

Mashed Sweet Potatoes

The gorgeous color of sweet potatoes makes this a lovely side dish with roast pork or beef. If you prefer a sweeter dish, add a bit more sugar to taste.

MAKES 3–4 SERVINGS

2 cups peeled and cubed sweet potatoes
Dash of salt
4 ounces cream cheese
¼ teaspoon each nutmeg, cinnamon, and ginger
1 tablespoon sugar

In a medium saucepan, boil the sweet potatoes in a small amount of salted water until fork tender. Drain off the liquid and leave the potatoes in the hot pot for about 5 minutes. Whisk in the cream cheese, spices, and sugar, stirring well until smooth.

—Courtenay L. Miller

Cℓ

Somebody Loves Sweet Potatoes

When my children were small, they helped prepare Thanksgiving dinner by grating sweet pota-

toes for this old family favorite. Once you try it, you may never go back to candied yams!

MAKES 6–8 SERVINGS

1 cup sugar
1 cup melted butter
½ cup half-and-half
2 teaspoons powdered ginger
1 tablespoon candied ginger, chopped fine
1 cup coarsely chopped pecans
4 cups grated raw sweet potatoes
¼ cup grated orange rind

Preheat the oven to 350 degrees. Grease a 9-inch baking dish. Combine the sugar, melted butter, half-and-half, powdered ginger, chopped ginger, and chopped pecans in a large bowl. Combine the potatoes and the orange rind in a medium bowl. Add the potato mixture to the butter mixture. Pour into the prepared dish and bake 20 to 30 minutes or until the potatoes are tender and all the liquid is absorbed.

—Jay Cooper

Cℓ

Candied Yams

The quick and easy way to make candied yams is to buy a big can of sweet potatoes in heavy syrup, pour the whole thing into a buttered baking dish, and top with miniature marshmallows.

This recipe requires slightly more work, but I trust you will find the results worth the effort.

MAKES 4–6 SERVINGS

4 large yellow yams or sweet potatoes, washed
    and peeled
1½ cups packed brown sugar
1 tablespoon cinnamon
1 teaspoon nutmeg
1 cup butter, cut into chunks
1 cup orange juice with pulp

Place the yams in a large saucepan, add water to cover, and boil until the yams are fork tender. Remove the yams from water and slice about 1 inch thick. Preheat the oven to 350 degrees. Grease a 9-by-13-inch baking dish. Combine the brown sugar, nutmeg, and cinnamon in a small bowl. Place a layer of yams in the prepared baking dish. Top with chunks of butter and some of the sugar mixture. Continue to layer yams, butter, and sugar mixture to fill the pan. Pour the orange juice over the mixture, sprinkle any remaining sugar mixture over the top, cover, and bake 20 to 30 minutes or until the potatoes are tender and glazed.

—Lauren Rhodes Cooper

Grandmother's Macaroni and Cheese

Comfort food of the first order, my grandmother's macaroni and cheese is a firm, sweet custard with plenty of cheese flavor that will remind you of visits to the Deep South.

MAKES 8–10 SERVINGS

1 (16-ounce) box dried elbow macaroni
½ cup butter
3 large eggs
1 (12-ounce) can evaporated milk
¼ cup sugar
1 teaspoon cayenne pepper
½ teaspoon salt
1½ pounds shredded sharp Cheddar cheese

Cook the macaroni according to package directions and drain well. Preheat the oven to 350 degrees. Put the butter in a 3-quart baking dish and place the dish in the oven until the butter melts. Beat the eggs with the milk, sugar, cayenne pepper, and salt. Toss the macaroni in the melted butter. Reserve 1 cup cheese and sprinkle the remainder over the macaroni. Pour the egg mixture over the macaroni, sprinkle with the remaining cheese, and bake 20 minutes or until the cheese is melted and the mixture is set.

Note: You can reduce the amount of sugar called for if you prefer the dish less sweet.

—Lottie Twyner Rhodes

Buttermilk Macaroni and Cheese

Rumor has it that no one can resist this deliciously creamy macaroni and cheese.

MAKES 8 SERVINGS

1 (16-ounce) box Kraft Deluxe Macaroni &
   Cheese Dinner
1½ cups buttermilk
1 (8-ounce) package cream cheese
½ stick (4 tablespoons) butter
3 large eggs
Salt and pepper to taste
4 ounces sharp Cheddar cheese, chopped into
   medium chunks
4 ounces sharp Cheddar cheese, shredded

Cook the macaroni according to package directions, reserving the package of Cheddar cheese. Rinse and drain. Preheat the oven to 350 degrees. Grease a 9-by-13-inch baking dish. In a saucepan, combine the buttermilk, cream cheese, the package of Cheddar from the box, and the butter. Cook on low heat to make a creamy sauce. Pour the drained macaroni into a large mixing bowl. Stir in the cheese sauce and beaten eggs, and season with salt and pepper to taste. Pour the mixture into the prepared baking dish, add the chopped cheese, and bake 45 minutes or until firm. Top with the shredded cheese and return the pan to the oven for 5 minutes or until the cheese melts. Let cool for 10 minutes before serving.

—Annetta Maria Thomas

White Bread and Oyster Stuffing

To everything there is a season. And the oyster season really does correspond to the months of the year containing the letter r, because May, June, July, and August are the months when oysters spawn. Oyster stuffing is best prepared during the colder months of the year. If you shuck your own oysters, reserve the liquid from the shucking in a bowl to flavor the stuffing.

MAKES 8–10 SERVINGS

½ cup plus 4 tablespoons butter
10 cups chopped stale white bread
1 cup chopped onions
1 cup finely chopped celery
3 pints oysters, with their liquor
2 teaspoons ground sage
Salt and pepper to taste
1 cup cream
1 cup freshly minced flat-leaf parsley
1 cup whole milk, as needed

Preheat the oven to 350 degrees. Melt the ½ cup butter in a 3-quart baking dish. Add the bread and toss to coat well. In a large skillet, melt 2 tablespoons of the remaining butter, and sauté the onions and celery until tender. Remove the vegetables from the pan. Drain the oysters, reserving the liquid. Chop the oysters into bite-sized pieces. Add the remaining 2 tablespoons of butter to the skillet and sauté the oysters until the edges curl slightly. Blend the ground sage, salt, and pepper into the re-served oyster liquor. Whip in the cream. Add the chopped oysters, any liquid remaining in the pan, and the minced parsley. Pour over the chopped bread and mix well. (Add milk if more liquid is needed to soften the bread so the mixture holds together.) Bake 30 minutes or until set. Serve with turkey or roast chicken.

—*Brenda Rhodes Miller*

C H A P T E R 5

One-Dish Meals

Saved! Sanctified! Fire Baptized! Washed in the Blood!
Filled with the Holy Ghost!

CHURCH LADIES AND THEIR PASTORS

Few relationships can match the intensity of a church lady's devotion to her pastor. He is viewed as God's representative on earth and therefore is an authority figure on matters both spiritual and temporal. When a church lady begins a statement with "Pastor said . . . ," you can be sure she expects no opposition.

The pastor of a church is expected to be a role model, a leader, and a servant of his congregation all tied up in one neat package. There are times when he must act as a surrogate father, a marriage counselor, and a mediator in family disputes.

No matter how many demands his congregation may make on his time and energy—not to mention his patience—he must always strive to maintain his composure and the demeanor of a Christian filled with compassion and love. Is it any wonder, then, that so many church ladies form strong attachments to their pastors?

While there are churches all over the country whose pastors are women, the great majority of

Ms. Virginia Strong and her sister, Mrs. Luevenia Combest,
escort their pastor, Rev. Courtenay L. Miller.

African American churches usually call men to be their leaders. Many churches insist the pastor be a *married* man to boot.

Some denominations officially prohibit women from being named as pastor, citing biblical precedent. In other denominations, however, it is simply tradition that keeps women from filling that role. But that is a subject for another story.

While the man of God is often called "Pastor," with no surname attached, within the African American church his duties include being not only the pastor but also the priest and the prophet of his congregation.

Pastor is simply the title that encompasses those functions. Rare is the man equally gifted in all three areas. Maybe that's why church ladies see their support as a vital ingredient in his success.

To be a pastor is to be a shepherd, tending to the members of the congregation diligently and lovingly even when they stray. As church folks weather the storms of life, it is the pastor to whom they turn.

This means the pastor is on call 24/7, always ready to visit the sick, to counsel the troubled in spirit, and to listen to the brokenhearted. Church ladies expect their pastor to show up in good times and in bad times, for everything from operations to birthday parties and anything in between.

The function of a priest is to administer the sacraments. He is charged with baptizing, marrying, blessing, and burying members of his congregation and their extended families.

Where it can get tricky is fulfilling the role of prophet. The prophet brings God's Word to God's people. In other words, he teaches and preaches.

Many a pastoral career rides on the Sunday morning sermon. Preaching is what people hear and remember. It is the centerpiece of the worship service. Church ladies come to have their spirits fed with the Word of God, and heaven help an otherwise wonderful pastor who can't preach.

"Maybe you should sing during your sermon," a church lady may advise her pastor. "I don't think you should tell any more jokes in your sermon," another will suggest.

"If you could just make your sermons shorter, you'd be better off," is the kind of friendly advice that might come on the same Sunday as, "I sure do wish you had delved into your text more deeply."

Obviously, it is nearly impossible to please every single church lady who offers her pastor advice on his preaching. Yet pastors all over the country do take heed of the church ladies' critiques because to ignore them is a recipe for disaster. In most cases, church ladies make up more than half the congregation, and they do an enormous amount of volunteer work, not to mention making financial contributions. They are a vocal constituency who must be heard. Pastors know this and, as a result, they do pay attention.

In the best case, the relationship between church ladies and their pastors is purely platonic in nature, unselfish, and nurturing. Church ladies happily share their wealth of experience, received wisdom, common sense, and everyday moral understanding with their pastor to help him in his ministry.

If he's smart, he accepts their help graciously. After all, many church ladies were part of the congregation before he got there and expect to remain part of it long after he's gone. Good as they are, church ladies are only human, so of course they can expect forgiveness if their advice sometimes includes the hint of a personal grudge or hidden bias.

It falls to the pastor, who must remain a man after God's own heart, always to model himself after the One who is Divine.

Some pastors are better at this than others. And therein lies another tale for another day.

Spectacular Last-Minute Dinner

If you've got dinner guests coming and only an hour to prepare, here's a dish that will look fabulous, taste great, and still leave you time to put on your lipstick before they arrive.

MAKES 8–10 SERVINGS

1½ pounds angel hair pasta
1 pound smoked sausage
2 boneless, skinless chicken breasts
1 (8-ounce) salmon fillet
Salt and pepper to taste
1 large yellow onion, chopped
4 cloves garlic, chopped
About 1 cup olive oil, as needed
1 pound mussels, washed and debearded
½ cup white wine
½ pound large shrimp, cleaned and deveined
3 pounds fresh spinach, washed
½ cup sesame oil
2 tablespoons toasted sesame seeds

Cook the angel hair pasta according to package directions. Drain and keep hot while you finish the recipe. Slice the sausage in ¼-inch rounds and cook in a cast-iron skillet. Set aside and keep warm. Season the chicken breasts and salmon fillet with salt and pepper to taste; drizzle with a small amount of olive oil, and broil in the oven until done. Cut the chicken breasts in strips and set aside. Break the salmon into large pieces and set aside.

Sauté the onion and garlic in a couple of tablespoons of the olive oil. Add the mussels to the onion and garlic mixture with a bit more olive oil and the wine. Shake the pan a few times, cover, and cook until the mussels open.

Slice the shrimp in half lengthwise, add them to the mussels, and cook for 4 minutes. Drain and reserve the liquid. Drop the spinach into boiling salted water and cook for 3 minutes. Drain the spinach and arrange it on a large platter; season to taste. When all the ingredients are cooked, toss the pasta in the sesame oil and arrange it on top of the spinach. Top the pasta with the shrimp, sliced chicken, sausage, and mussels. Add the salmon, top with the toasted sesame seeds, and drizzle the reserved liquid over the pasta. Serve with a green salad and bread for a complete meal.

—Brenda Rhodes Miller

Veggie Lasagna

Every church supper should offer meatless entrees because every church has vegetarians in the congregation. This is a delicious alternative to meat.

MAKES 8–10 SERVINGS

1 (16-ounce) package lasagna noodles
Olive oil, as needed
2 teaspoons minced garlic

1 medium onion, diced

1 (16-ounce) package fresh sliced mushrooms

1 medium eggplant, peeled and cut into ½-inch-thick slices

1 (10-ounce) package frozen artichoke hearts, thawed and sliced

1 (16-ounce) jar spaghetti sauce of your choice

1 (16-ounce) can diced tomatoes

½ cup sun-dried tomatoes, cut into thin strips

½ teaspoon garlic salt

¼ teaspoon cinnamon

¼ teaspoon cumin

Dash of pepper

Dash of oregano

Dash of basil

1 (8-ounce) container low-fat cottage cheese

1 (8-ounce) container low-fat ricotta cheese

2 (10-ounce) packages frozen spinach, thawed and drained

¾ cup freshly grated Parmesan cheese

2 (10-ounce) packages mozzarella cheese slices

Cook 8 lasagna noodles according to the package directions and set aside on paper towels. In a large, deep skillet, heat the ¼ cup of olive oil, and sauté the garlic and onion over medium heat for 5 minutes. Add the mushrooms and sauté for about 8 minutes. Add the eggplant and artichoke hearts, and sauté until tender. Stir in the spaghetti sauce, diced tomatoes, sun-dried tomatoes, and the seasonings, and simmer for 20 minutes. Combine the cottage cheese and ricotta cheese in a medium bowl. Preheat the oven to 375 degrees. Lightly spread a coating of the sauce on the bottom of a 9-by-13-inch baking dish, then lay half the noodles in the pan and coat with the cheese mixture. Add another layer of sauce and top that with half the spinach. Sprinkle with Parmesan cheese and top with half the mozzarella slices. Repeat the layers, ending with the remaining mozzarella cheese. Bake for 45 minutes. Let stand 10 minutes, then cut, serve, and enjoy.

—Shawn Cooper

Red Beans and Rice

According to custom along the Gulf Coast, red beans and rice make the perfect Monday dinner because the dish will cook quite happily on the back of the stove while one attends to other chores. My mother often added shrimp to the basic recipe that follows here.

MAKES 4–6 SERVINGS

1 pound dried red kidney beans

1 pound sausage, cut into 2-inch rounds

6 cloves garlic, chopped fine

2 onions, coarsely chopped

1 green bell pepper, coarsely chopped

3 ribs celery with leaves, coarsely chopped

Salt and pepper to taste

3 cups cooked white rice

Wash the red beans and remove any debris and broken beans. In a Dutch oven, lightly brown the sausage. Sauté the vegetables with the sausage for 5 to 6 minutes. Add the beans and cover with about 3 inches of water; mix well. Cook, covered, on low, adding water as needed until the beans are tender. Taste and add salt and pepper as needed. Serve over the rice.

—Carolyn Bolden Rhodes

Mexican Lunch

Mrs. Cornell Sharperson recalls serving this delightful dish along with a pot of cabbage and a pan of cornbread to her son and his friends when they visited her on leave from the Air Force many years ago. She got rave reviews and so will you.

MAKES 4 SERVINGS

1 pound ground beef
1 cup diced onion
1 cup diced green bell pepper
2 cups canned tomatoes
1¾ cups buttermilk or 2 cups sour cream
2 cups uncooked macaroni
1 tablespoon sugar
1 tablespoon chili powder
1 teaspoon salt

Cook the ground beef, onion, and green pepper in a large skillet until the beef is brown. Add the tomatoes, buttermilk, macaroni, sugar, chili powder, and salt. Simmer for 20 minutes or until the macaroni is tender.

—Mrs. Cornell Sharperson

String Beans with Smoked Turkey and White Potatoes

It seems a shame to serve limp, canned string beans when fresh ones are available. If cutting off the tips and pulling out the strings from several pounds of fresh string beans is too much trouble for you, by all means use three bags of frozen beans. The sugar brings out the natural sweetness of string beans. Cook just until tender so the bright green color of the beans remains.

MAKES 6 SERVINGS

1 cup smoked turkey, cut into bite-sized pieces
3 pounds fresh or frozen whole string beans
1 fresh lemon
¼ teaspoon sugar
2 large white potatoes peeled, cubed, and parboiled
Salt and pepper to taste

Bring 6 quarts of water to a boil in a covered pot. Remove the lid, add the smoked turkey, and continue to boil for about 10 minutes. Place the string beans in a bowl and squeeze the lemon juice over them. Toss the beans in the juice then add them to the boiling water. Sprinkle the sugar over beans and stir. Cover and cook for about 10 minutes on medium heat. Add the parboiled potatoes and cook for another 10 to 12 minutes. Taste and season with salt and pepper as needed.

Note: You can substitute ham or bacon for the turkey, if desired.

—Reverend Clarence Earl Miller

Ce

Chicken and Noodles

Small, light dumplings take some practice to prepare. If you haven't yet mastered homemade dumplings, use this recipe to make a satisfying and delicious meal reminiscent of the best chicken and dumpling one-dish dinners.

MAKES 6–8 SERVINGS

¼ cup vegetable oil
4 pounds chicken wings and thighs, rinsed and drained well
Goyaobo seasoning with pepper to taste
1 cup chopped celery
1 cup chopped carrots
1 cup frozen English peas with pearl onions
4 cups chicken broth

3 teaspoons chopped fresh basil
1 (16-ounce) package egg noodles

Heat the oil in a Dutch oven. Sprinkle the chicken parts with the adobo seasoning, tossing to cover all sides. Brown the chicken in the oil, then stir in the vegetables and chicken broth. Cook over low heat for 20 minutes. Add the basil and noodles and stir well. Add water to cover and cook until the noodles are done.

—Lolita Cusic

Ce

Chicken and Rice Casserole

Easy to prepare and satisfying to eat, this casserole can be made ahead and frozen to have on hand for unexpected guests or an impromptu church committee meeting.

MAKES 6–8 SERVINGS

2 (10½-ounce) cans cream of chicken, cream of mushroom, or cream of celery soup
2–3 cups milk
4 cups uncooked rice
1 (10-ounce) package frozen sweet peas
1 teaspoon summer savory
2 teaspoons black pepper
3 tablespoons oil
1 whole chicken, cut into parts

Great Is Thy Faithfulness

MRS. CORNELL SHARPERSON
BETHLEHEM BAPTIST CHURCH
SPOTSYLVANIA, VIRGINIA

The church secretary forwarded a telephone message to me in early March. A Mrs. Cornell Sharperson of Spotsylvania, Virginia, had left her phone number. She wanted someone to call and tell her how to get a copy of my first cookbook, *The Church Ladies' Divine Desserts*.

As soon as I heard Mrs. Sharperson's lovely Southern voice, it was like old home week, as my mother used to say. When I asked her what had prompted her to call, she chuckled as she told me she still had the December 2001 article from the *Washington Post* about my book.

Mrs. Cornell Sharperson of Spotsylvania, Virginia.

Spotsylvania is quite a ways from Washington, D.C., so I just had to know how she came to have that article in the first place.

"Were you born in Washington?" I asked.

Although she was born and raised in Chatham, Virginia, Mrs. Sharperson told me that she and her husband had once lived in Washington, D.C.

"We are members of Jones United Methodist Church on G Street, SE, and when we moved to Spotsylvania, we would drive an hour and half to go to church every Sunday. I used to sing with the United Gospel Stars."

I was astonished by such faithfulness and inquired whether they still commuted for Sunday services. She told me her family had now been in Spotsylvania for more than thirty years, and she joined Bethlehem Baptist Church under watch care in order to have a place of worship closer to home.

"Watch care" allows for all the rights and privileges of membership and implies that the person under watch care will one day return to his or her home church.

Mrs. Sharperson was warm and gracious as we chatted about one thing and another until our conversation eventually turned to our families.

From the *Post* article she already knew that my husband is the pastor of Norbeck Community

Church, and she gently teased me about being "first lady." I laughed along with her and then we talked about children.

Her oldest son went to the Naval Academy in Annapolis, Maryland, and her daughter recently opened a shop called Simply Sweet on Route 3 in Fredericksburg, where "they do wedding cakes and all occasion cakes by special order."

The shop also sells cake supplies. Talking about cakes got us off the subject of children before she could tell me about her other two, and we started talking about cooking.

Mrs. Sharperson loves to cook. She herself has made wedding cakes and special occasion cakes for years, so it's easy to see where her daughter came by her talent.

When I told her that I was writing a new cookbook and begged her for a recipe to include in it, she most graciously obliged by sending me several.

Just before we hung up, I remembered that the Twyner branch of my family had once held its reunion in Spotsylvania. "I have family in Spotsylvania," I said. "Do you know any Twyners?"

To my surprise, she knew them well. In fact, her children had gone to school with the children of my cousins George Henry and Lynne Twyner.

Several days later Mrs. Sharperson and I talked again. This time she asked me what I knew about panorama eggs. The name didn't ring a bell. "The sugar eggs with scenes inside. I'm sure you've seen one."

Had I ever. When I was a little girl in Alabama, my godparents, John and Joyce Irons, gave me just such an egg for Easter. I'd just never known that it had a special name. What I do remember is how it sort of melted away after a few days of constant attention from me. Were my hot hands or the humid weather to blame?

"I'll make you one and send it for Easter," Mrs. Sharperson promised.

I was astounded. A person could actually make those sugar eggs? Who knew? And then she gave me an even greater gift. She told me the secret of keeping my panorama egg intact so I could enjoy it year after year: Keep it tightly covered and store it in a cool, dry place. When the promised egg arrived, I handled it carefully and peered inside. The three-dimensional scene was as magical as I'd remembered from childhood.

Only now, thanks to Mrs. Sharperson, my egg will last long past Easter week.

Preheat the oven to 350 degrees. In a large bowl, combine the cream soup and 2 cups of the milk. Stir in the rice, peas, savory, and pepper. Pour the oil into a 9-by-13-inch glass baking dish and swirl it to coat the dish.

Pour the soup and rice mixture into the dish, and lay the chicken pieces on top.

Cover with foil and bake for 30 minutes. If all the liquid is absorbed before the chicken and rice are cooked, add more milk as needed. Remove the foil and bake for 20 minutes or until the chicken is golden brown.

—Lauren Cooper

Cℓℓ

Chicken or Turkey Casserole

This easy casserole travels well and would be the perfect dish to take to a church potluck supper.

MAKES 6–8 SERVINGS

1 (3-pound) chicken or 3 pounds of turkey parts
1 (10¾-ounce) can cream of chicken soup
1 (10¾-ounce) can celery soup
Chicken stock, reserved from cooking the chicken
½ cup margarine
1 small onion, chopped fine
1 (16-ounce) package herb seasoned stuffing

Lay the chicken or turkey in a Dutch oven and add water to cover. Boil until tender. Drain, and reserve the stock. When cool enough to handle, remove the meat from the bones and cut it into chunks. Combine the soups and in a large bowl. Measure 2 soup cans full of reserved stock and add them to the soups. Melt the margarine in a small skillet. In a medium bowl, combine the melted margarine with the onion and stuffing. Preheat the oven to 350 degrees. Place a layer of chicken on the bottom of a baking dish. Cover with a layer of soup mixture and then a layer of stuffing mixture. Continue to layer until all ingredients are used, ending with the soup mixture.

Bake 30 to 45 minutes or until heated through. Serve with Cranberry Salad (pages 42–3).

—Mrs. Cornell Sharperson

Cℓℓ

Taco Chicken

This never-fail recipe comes from Southern California. Serve it with rice and an avocado-tomato salad for a complete meal.

MAKES 4 SERVINGS

1 pound chicken, cut into pieces
1 (2-ounce) package taco seasoning
1 oven cooking bag

Wash and drain the chicken pieces. Add the taco mix to the cooking bag and shake to blend.

Put the chicken in the bag and add liquid as directed.

Cook according to the package directions.

—*Madeliene Doris Douglas*

Ce

Shepherd's Pie

This is a popular meal for growing boys. Not only does it fill them up, but they can also enjoy making it for themselves.

MAKES 6–8 SERVINGS

6 medium potatoes
¼ cup butter
⅔ cup milk
⅔ cup ranch dressing
1 pound ground beef
1 (16-ounce) bag of frozen vegetables
Onion powder, salt, and pepper to taste

Peel the potatoes and cut them into large chunks. Transfer them to a medium saucepan, add water to cover, and boil until tender. Drain the potatoes, add the butter, milk, and salad dressing, and mash to a smooth consistency. Brown the ground beef in a large skillet. Add the vegetables and cook over medium heat until warmed through. Add

the onion powder, salt, and pepper to taste. Preheat the oven to 375 degrees. Spread the meat and vegetable mixture evenly over the bottom of a 9-by-13-inch baking dish. Top with the potatoes and bake for 10 minutes.

—*Jacqueline A. Duodu*

Ce

Turkey Divan

When you're faced with a mountain of leftover turkey, use it in this lovely dish. In fact, you may want to roast a bigger-than-usual turkey just so you'll have plenty on hand in the freezer.

MAKES 4 SERVINGS

Vegetable cooking spray
3 tablespoons butter
3 tablespoons all-purpose flour
2¼ cups milk
1½ tablespoons mustard
3 cups fresh or frozen broccoli flowerets
3 cups chopped cooked turkey or chicken
1 cup freshly grated Parmesan cheese
½ cup unflavored bread crumbs

Preheat the oven to 400 degrees. Spray a 9-inch baking dish with cooking spray.

In a saucepan, combine the butter and flour, stirring and cooking to make a paste or a roux. Stir in the milk and continue cooking until smooth. Stir in the mustard and remove from the heat. Place a layer of broccoli, then a layer of turkey in the prepared baking dish. Sprinkle with the cheese. Continue layering until all the broccoli and turkey are used up. Pour the sauce over the top and sprinkle with the breadcrumbs. Bake 30 minutes or until brown and bubbly.

—Melanie Shelwood

Ce

Turkey Wings with Root Vegetables

Low-cost turkey wings are not glamorous but they can make a substantial and satisfying midwinter meal. Sweet potatoes, carrots, and celery play off nicely against the unctuous flavor of these slow-baked wings.

MAKES 3–4 SERVINGS

1 tablespoon salt
1 tablespoon pepper
1 teaspoon sage
1 teaspoon garlic powder
⅛ teaspoon cinnamon
6 whole turkey wings, each cut into three pieces
¼ cup safflower oil
2 cups coarsely chopped celery with leaves
2 cups coarsely chopped carrots

2 cups peeled and coarsely chopped sweet potatoes
4 cloves garlic, sliced

Preheat the oven to 350 degrees. Mix the seasonings in a small bowl. Rub the seasoning mix on all sides of the wings. Heat half the oil in a large skillet and brown the wings. Transfer the browned wings to a baking dish, top with the vegetables and garlic, and drizzle with the remaining oil. Cover with foil and bake for 35 minutes. Turn the turkey parts, recover with foil, and continue baking for 20 minutes longer. Remove the foil and bake an additional 10 minutes. Serve the wings with the vegetables.

—Mrs. Bessie Brazley

Ce

Heartwarming Neck Bones

Pork neck bones cooked with vegetables and rice make for a hearty, inexpensive meal just perfect to serve on a cold winter's day. The alcohol in the tequila cooks off while giving the neck bones an unforgettable flavor.

MAKES 6–8 SERVINGS

5 pounds meaty pork neck bones
Salt and pepper to taste
2 tablespoons canola oil
1 tablespoon chopped garlic

1 cup chopped celery

1 cup chopped green bell pepper

1½ cups sliced onions

1 (14½-ounce) can chopped Italian tomatoes

1½ cups hot water

½ cup tequila

2 cups white potatoes cut into large chunks

4 leaves fresh sage, chopped fine

1 cup frozen peas and carrots

1 (5-ounce) package instant seasoned rice,
*   such as Mahatma*

Sprinkle the neck bones with salt and pepper. Heat the canola oil in a Dutch oven and cook the bones in the oil until brown on all sides. Add the garlic, celery, bell pepper, and onions and cook until fragrant, stirring frequently. Add the tomatoes with their liquid and stir in the hot water and tequila. Reduce the heat, cover, and simmer for 1½ hours. Add the potatoes and continue cooking until the meat is so tender it falls from the bones. Use tongs to remove the large bones. Discard the bones or serve them to your favorite dog. Cook the rice according to package directions, adding the frozen peas and carrots at the beginning of the cooking time. Fluff with a fork when done. Ladle the neck bones into individual bowls and top each serving with ¼ cup of the rice mixture.

—*Brenda Rhodes Miller*

Simple South of the Border Casserole

This dish is easy to prepare because it "doctors up" ready-made ingredients. Feel free to substitute your own homemade chili if you prefer.

MAKES 6 SERVINGS

1 (16-ounce) can red kidney beans

1 (15-ounce) can chili without beans

1 small yellow onion, chopped fine

6 green onion tops, chopped (reserve about
*   ¼ cup for garnish)*

1 large clove garlic, minced

1 teaspoon cumin

Salt and pepper to taste

2 (15½-ounce) cans tamales (remove the
*   paper from the tamales)*

1 large yellow onion, thinly sliced (optional)

1 (16-ounce) package shredded sharp
*   Cheddar cheese*

1 (10-ounce) bag Fritos

2 tablespoons vegetable oil

1 cup sour cream

Preheat the oven to 350 degrees. Drain the kidney beans and reserve the liquid. Combine the beans, chili, chopped yellow and green onions, garlic, and cumin in a medium bowl. Taste and season with salt and pepper as needed. (Remember, the Fritos are salty so go easy on the salt.) Slice the tamales in half lengthwise and place a single layer on the bot-

Grow Where You're Planted

EVELENA SCOTT HUDSON
FLAT ROCK BAPTIST CHURCH
MATTHEWS, GEORGIA

Evelena Scott was born the day after Valentine's Day 1898, the sixth child of Richard and Liza Scott. At the tender age of fourteen she married Elbert Hudson, a man twenty-five years her senior. Their family grew to include twenty children, with fifteen of them growing up to have children of their own.

Times were hard, and as the children came of age they joined Mr. Hudson working in the fields. Mrs. Hudson did just about everything else.

The multitalented Mrs. Evelena Scott Hudson belonged to Flat Rock Baptist Church.

According to her granddaughter, Joyce Clemons, Mrs. Hudson was the family's disciplinarian, laundress, kitchen yard gardener, and doctor.

She made her family's clothes as well as all the bed linens on a Singer foot-pedal sewing machine. Just about the only store-bought items of apparel in her household were shoes and her one vanity, her special church hats decorated with feathered plumes.

Her remedies came from her garden, the kitchen, and the great outdoors. To cut a fever, Mrs. Hudson put gypsum weed on the patient's forearms and forehead. Spider webs covered open wounds to stop the bleeding. If someone stepped on a nail, "Dr. Hudson" would cut a slice of fat back and place the salty side over the puncture to prevent blood poisoning.

However, her greatest household skill was cooking. Renowned for her culinary abilities, she cooked what she grew in her garden.

What she didn't cook right away she "put up" for lean times. Canned vegetables and a full assortment of fruit jellies and preserves lined her shelves. With milk from the family cow she churned her own butter. And she tended a chicken yard.

Unshakeable faith was the basis of her boundless energy and her determination to make a good life for herself and her family. By any measure, Evelena Scott Hudson did the best she could with what she had been given.

God asks no more than that of anyone.

tom of a 9-by-13-inch baking dish. Layer the sliced onions, if desired, the cheese, chili mixture, and Fritos over the tamales. Continue layering until all the ingredients are used, ending with a layer of Fritos. Whisk together the kidney bean liquid and the vegetable oil. Drizzle the mixture over the top of the casserole. Bake, covered, for 30 minutes. Uncover and bake an additional 15 minutes. Serve with sour cream on the side. Enjoy with a salad or fresh fruit.

—Marshel O'Shields

Beef Short Ribs with Orzo

During one of the coldest winters on record, my family craved comfort food. This recipe makes for a rich and substantial meal using low-cost ingredients.

MAKES 8–10 SERVINGS

4½ pounds beef short ribs
Salt and pepper to taste
1 medium red onion, sliced
1 large yellow onion, sliced
1 tablespoon minced garlic
1½ cups apple juice
1 teaspoon minced fresh ginger
1 teaspoon celery seed

6 whole sage leaves
1 beef bouillon cube
2 tablespoons apple cider vinegar
¼ cup red wine
2 cups chopped carrots
4 medium white potatoes with their skins, cut into chunks
1 cup orzo or rice

Heat a Dutch oven. Salt and pepper all sides of the short ribs and brown them in the hot Dutch oven. When the short ribs are brown on all sides, remove them from the Dutch oven. Add the onions and garlic to the pan juices and sauté until tender. If there is not enough liquid, add some of the apple juice at this time. When the vegetables are tender, add the apple juice (or the remaining apple juice), the ginger, celery seed, and sage. Bring the mixture to a low boil and add the bouillon cube. When the bouillon cube is dissolved, taste and adjust seasonings. Add the vinegar and red wine and stir to blend. Return the short ribs to the Dutch oven, reduce the heat, and cook, covered, on low heat for 1 hour. Add the carrots and potatoes and cook 30 more minutes or until the short ribs are very tender. Remove any bones, add the orzo, and cook until the pasta is done. Taste, adjust the seasonings, and serve with a green vegetable.

Note: If you're cutting down on carbohydrates, cook the dish without the potatoes.

—Brenda Rhodes Miller

Stuffed Peppers

Basically, this is meatloaf cooked in a casing. The bright color of the peppers and tomato sauce raises plain meatloaf to new heights. To make your own bread crumbs, toast stale or leftover bread in a 300-degree oven until dry. Transfer them to a plastic bag and crush them with a rolling pin.

MAKES 8 SERVINGS

8 large whole red, green, and yellow bell peppers
1 pound ground beef
1 pound sage pork sausage
1 cup bread crumbs, homemade or store-bought
2 large eggs, beaten well
1 cup cooked rice
1/2 cup tomato sauce
1 small onion, finely chopped
2 cloves garlic, minced
1 teaspoon summer savory
1/2 teaspoon thyme
Salt and pepper to taste
1/4 cup vegetable oil
1/2 cup melted butter

Preheat the oven to 350 degrees. Slice the tops off of the bell peppers and remove the ribs and seeds. Do not discard the tops. Combine the meats, bread crumbs, eggs, rice, tomato sauce, onion, garlic, and seasonings in a large bowl; mix well.

Pour the oil into a 9-by-12-inch baking dish and swirl to coat the bottom. Stand the peppers in the dish and fill them with the meat mixture. Replace the tops and drizzle with the melted butter. Bake 45 to 55 minutes or until the filling is done and the bell peppers are soft.

—Carolyn Bolden Rhodes

A Little Different Casserole

Eggplant and olives give this simple casserole an exotic flavor. If you prefer, you can substitute turkey sausage for the pork. Increase the quantity of olive oil to 1/4 cup. Put half in bottom of casserole and drizzle the rest over the meat mixture.

MAKES 6 SERVINGS

2 tablespoons olive oil
1 pound fresh green beans, washed, stemmed, and cut into bite-sized pieces
1/2 pound eggplant, peeled and sliced very thin
Salt and pepper to taste
1 1/2 pounds ground pork sausage
1 (8-ounce) can tomato sauce
1 teaspoon minced garlic
1/2 teaspoon cinnamon
1/4 cup chopped black and green olives
2 large eggs
12 ounces ricotta cheese
1/2 cup freshly grated Parmesan cheese

Reaching Out While Reaching In

ANNE ANDERSON PAULIN

OLD ST. ANDREWS EPISCOPAL CHURCH
BLOOMFIELD, CONNECTICUT

*A*nne Paulin grew up in Toomsuba, Mississippi, with her extended family around her. She remembers her town as being more like a village than anything else. Now she lives in Connecticut where childhood lessons serve her well.

Mrs. Paulin has been a member of her small church for nearly thirty years, serving on the vestry or governing body, singing in the choir, and doing work with Episcopal Church Women. Everyone has at least one role if not several to fulfill, and in-reach as well as out-reach is encouraged.

Most of us are familiar with outreach, which involves helping to meet the needs of the community outside the church in ways such as building homes for the homeless through Habitat for Humanity.

Ecumenical in their ministry, Old St. Andrews supports the efforts of the Catholic Worker group that runs St. Bridget's House, which runs a food bank and also provides inner-city children from Hartford with after-school and weekend programs, summer camp, and tutors. In-reach, on the other hand, helps people within the church who are temporarily in need. This might mean visiting people who are homebound, in hospitals, or in long-term care facilities. Church ladies also prepare meals, drive members to medical appointments, and deliver prescriptions.

"I don't know how people manage who don't have a church to support them with helping hands and prayers," says Mrs. Paulin.

Her philosophy is always to be involved, and she derives a sense of purpose from doing whatever good she can while she's here.

"The world is small and getting smaller all the time. Our neighbors can be anywhere in this world and we must help them," she believes.

Preheat the oven to 350 degrees. Coat the bottom of a 9-inch baking dish with the olive oil. Spread the beans in the bottom of the pan. Place the thinly sliced eggplant in a colander, sprinkle it with salt, and let the liquid drain out. Brown the sausage in a medium skillet and drain off the excess fat. Add the tomato sauce, garlic, and cinnamon to the sausage, and spread the mixture over the green beans. Pat the eggplant dry and layer the slices over the meat mixture. Sprinkle the chopped olives over the eggplant. Blend the eggs and ricotta cheese in a small bowl; add salt and pepper to taste, and spread the egg and cheese mixture over the olives. Top with Parmesan cheese and bake 35 minutes.

—Jacqueline A. Duodo

Ce

Keep-It-Simple Quiche

There is no longer any debate about whether or not real men eat quiche. They do. And they will most likely ask for seconds on this one! Remember that country ham is very salty.

MAKES 4–6 SERVINGS

3 tablespoons vegetable oil
1 cup finely chopped onion
¼ cup finely chopped celery
¼ cup finely chopped green bell pepper
4 large eggs
2 cups evaporated milk

1 teaspoon nutmeg
¼ cup minced fresh flat-leaf parsley
¼ teaspoon pepper
1 cup chopped country ham
1 (9-inch) unbaked deep-dish pie shell
1 cup shrimp, crabmeat, or shredded white fish
1 cup shredded Swiss cheese

Preheat the oven to 350 degrees. Heat a skillet and add the oil. Sauté the onion until it is golden, then add the celery and bell pepper and sauté until soft. In a medium bowl, whisk together the eggs, milk, nutmeg, parsley, and pepper until well blended. Spread the country ham over the bottom of the pie shell. Layer the shrimp, crabmeat, or shredded white fish over the ham. Add the cooked vegetables. Sprinkle the Swiss cheese over the vegetables and pour the egg and milk mixture over top. Bake about 55 minutes or until the mixture is bubbling and the cheese has melted and browned slightly. Remove from the oven and let stand 5 minutes before slicing. Serve with a green salad or a fresh fruit salad.

—Leslie Williams

Ce

She's an On-Time Friend

JACQUELINE DUODU
BETHEL AME CHURCH
COPIAGUE, NEW YORK

Church ladies can appear in any form. Like angels unaware, they come in many guises and in a wide variety of shapes, sizes, and ages. Like the God they serve, church ladies may not come when you want them, but they're always right on time. They are on-time friends, yes, they are.*

Jackie Duodu, a member of Bethel AME, founded in 1814 and the oldest African American church on Long Island, recently brought those words to life for me.

Ms. Duodu is a recent graduate of Spelman College, where she majored in English with a drama minor. Currently a Hofstra graduate student, Jackie recently displayed her true colors as a dyed-in-the-wool church lady when a former dorm mate lost a beloved grandmother whom Jackie had known well.

Without batting an eye, Jackie e-mailed her Spelman sisters, informing them of their friend's loss. Then, she sent a blooming orchid to the family.

Not missing a beat, she packed her black dress and drove from Long Island to Brooklyn, where her friend lived. Loading up her car with comfort food, she drove her friend from Brooklyn to Washington, D.C., for the funeral.

And her kindness didn't stop there. Over several difficult days, Jackie pitched in with food preparation and housekeeping chores to help lighten the load for the grieving family.

At the funeral, she passed out programs and collected cards from floral arrangements so thank-you notes could be written. And throughout it all, she maintained her cheerful yet sympathetic manner.

People often speculate grimly on the future of the black church. Their hand-wringing, brow-beating, and lamentations fail to take into account young church ladies like Jacqueline Duodu.

As long as women of faith, whatever their age, continue to do good deeds without hesitation or any expectation of reward, the future of the black church will be secure.

*Adapted from the popular hymn "He's an On-Time God."

Madly Delicious Meatballs and Spaghetti

This recipe originally called for using a pressure cooker, but most people prefer making it in a Dutch oven, watching it carefully so the sauce does not burn.

MAKES 6–8 SERVINGS

MEATBALLS

1 pound ground chuck

½ pound ground pork

1 teaspoon chopped fresh basil

1 teaspoon black pepper

1 large egg

4 cloves garlic

1½ cups seasoned bread crumbs

1 teaspoon salt

5 teaspoons freshly grated Romano cheese

½ teaspoon baking powder

6 tablespoons canned evaporated milk

SPAGHETTI SAUCE

1 pint tomato juice

1 cup tomato sauce

1 (3-ounce) can tomato paste

¼ teaspoon chopped fresh basil

1 tablespoon freshly grated Romano cheese

Salt and pepper to taste

1 (16-ounce) box of your favorite pasta, cooked according to package directions

In a medium bowl, mix all the ingredients for the meatballs until thoroughly combined. Preheat the oven to 400 degrees. Pinch off golf ball–sized pieces of meat mixture and roll it into balls. Cook on a baking sheet about 10 minutes or until the meatballs are browned; turn over and cook 5 minutes longer. (You can also cook the meatballs in a skillet, turning them frequently until well browned.) Combine all the ingredients for the sauce in a Dutch oven. Cook for 18 to 25 minutes, adjusting the seasoning as needed. If the sauce is too thin, shake 1 teaspoon of flour into cold water and stir into the sauce until the flour is cooked. Add the meatballs to the sauce and cook for about 10 minutes. Serve over the cooked pasta with a large green salad and garlic bread.

Note: Experiment with additional herbs and spices for the sauce, perhaps adding garlic salt, oregano, or rosemary as desired.

—Marshel O'Shields

A Colorful Christmas Creole

This is a once-a-year dish that makes everyone look forward to Christmas! According to Maretta Brown-Miller, the recipe has made her a celebrity with her own family. She reports that while making the Christmas Creole is fun, it does take a lot of time and patience. She advises adapting the recipe with your own touches, such as adding smoked sausage or ham.

MAKES 10–12 SERVINGS

1/2 cup olive oil

2 medium yellow onions, chopped

1/2 cup chopped white onion

1/2 cup chopped red onion

1 large green bell pepper, chopped

1 large yellow bell pepper, chopped

1 large red bell pepper, chopped

4 stalks celery, chopped

1/2 teaspoon minced garlic

1 quart chicken broth

3–4 (14.5-ounce) cans crushed tomatoes
    with garlic

1 pound fresh mushrooms, cleaned and
    sliced

1 pound bean sprouts

1 teaspoon salt

1 teaspoon seasoned salt

1/2 teaspoon ground red pepper

1/2 teaspoon ground white pepper

5 bay leaves

1 tablespoon minced fresh basil

1 tablespoon minced fresh flat-leaf parsley

1 tablespoon minced fresh thyme

1 cup chopped flat-leaf parsley

1 1/2 teaspoons sugar

3 pounds fresh shrimp, without the heads,
    peeled and deveined

1 pound crab legs

Heat the olive oil in a large Dutch oven over medium-high heat. Add the onions, bell peppers, celery, and garlic and sauté, stirring often, for 15 to 20 minutes or until tender. Add the chicken broth and stir in the tomatoes, mushrooms, bean sprouts, salt and seasoned salt, red and white peppers, herbs, and sugar. Simmer for about 1 hour, stirring occasionally. Add the shrimp and crab legs and cook just until the shrimp are pink.

—Maretta Brown-Miller

Deep-Sea Casserole

The vivacious Mrs. Bull lives in St. Petersburg and swears by fresh Florida seafood for this casserole. If fresh lump crabmeat has too steep a price tag where you live, substitute frozen flaked cod or whiting.

MAKES 4–6 SERVINGS

1/2 cup butter

1 pound medium shrimp peeled, deveined,
    and sliced in half lengthwise

6 large hardboiled eggs, peeled and sliced

1 pound lump crabmeat or imitation crabmeat

1 cup milk

1 (26-ounce) can cream of shrimp or cream
    of mushroom soup

1 pound Cheddar cheese, grated

2 cups unflavored bread crumbs

Preheat the oven to 400 degrees. Grease a 9-inch baking dish with some of the butter. Cut the rest of the butter into small cubes. Layer the shrimp, then the sliced eggs, and then the crabmeat in the prepared baking dish. Continue layering until the ingredients are used. Combine the milk and soup in a medium bowl and pour the mixture over the other ingredients. Poke around with a knife to be sure the soup goes through all the layers. Cover with the cheese, top with the bread crumbs, and sprinkle the butter cubes on top. Bake 20 to 30 minutes until lightly brown on top and bubbly. Serve with salad or fruit.

—*Mrs. Rubye Smith Bull*

Ce

Afternoon Delight

This is a lovely supper dish that can also be dressed up to serve for teatime.

MAKES 4 SERVINGS

1 box of 8 frozen puff pastry shells
1 (10½-ounce) can cream of shrimp soup
2 tablespoons cream
1 cup shrimp, cooked, peeled, and deveined
½ cup tasso ham cubed (you can substitute good-quality deli ham)
1½ cups cooked and sliced potatoes
Creole seasoning, to taste

Bake the puff pastry shells according to package directions. Remove the tops and allow the shells to cool. Pour the soup into a small saucepan, add the cream, and blend. Add the shrimp, ham, and potatoes, and cook over medium heat until all ingredients are warmed through. Remove from the heat and add Creole seasoning to taste. (Remember, both the shrimp and the ham are salty, so go easy on the seasoning.) Fill the shells with the shrimp mixture, replace the pastry tops, and serve.

—*Brenda Rhodes Miller*

Ce

Eggplant and Crab Bake

Eggplant is actually a fruit that masquerades as a versatile vegetable. Its flavor is complemented by tomatoes, cheese, onion, and, in this recipe, shellfish. Pick nice, firm eggplants with fresh-looking green stems.

MAKES 4 ENTRÉE SERVINGS OR
8–10 APPETIZER SERVINGS

2 large eggplants
Olive oil
1 pound claw crabmeat
1 large egg beaten with a little cold water
1½ cups unflavored bread crumbs
½ teaspoon celery salt
Pepper to taste

Homecoming on the Grounds

At a church picnic one summer, someone made a passing reference to the oppressive heat. An elderly deacon took the remark as a challenge.

"Hot? Why, you don't know what hot is," he proclaimed. "I can tell you a little something about hot weather."

Warming to his topic, he proceeded to reminisce about the annual Homecoming held each summer on the grounds of his boyhood church. It was a time when people came from all over to reunite with friends and families.

"Folks who hadn't been heard from in years came to Homecoming. Even those that lived up north would come back. It was something."

Of course, church ladies took care of the food. Everything had to be prepared at home and brought to the church because there was not only no kitchen but no running water either. The deacons set up tables outside for the big meal, which was served mid-afternoon. "You've never seen so many cakes in all your life."

The schedule for the day included Sunday school followed by morning worship, then a break for dinner, and finally the afternoon program. Everyone who could get there crammed into the church for service.

"It was the hottest day of the summer, and our little church was packed. There wasn't room enough for a breeze to blow inside, let alone room to move around. Our preacher was on fire so he was right long-winded. He preached so hard the sweat was just flying off him. His preaching got the Saints so full up with the Holy Ghost they took to fainting left and right."

In order to get the fainting people some fresh air, they were laid on shutters to be "pallbearered out" through the church windows.

"When it was a lady going out, the nurses made sure her dress decently covered her legs. When it was a man, they made sure he had his hat."

Good thinking.

Preheat the oven to 325 degrees. Wash the eggplants and cut off the green stems. Cut the eggplants in half the long way, and brush the cut sides with olive oil. Place them, cut side down, on a cookie sheet and bake until the eggplant is soft when pierced with a fork. Set aside to cool. Increase the oven temperature to 350 degrees. Coat a 9-inch baking dish with olive oil. Scoop out the cooled eggplant flesh and mash it in a bowl. Pick through the crabmeat to remove any bits of shell. Add the crabmeat, beaten egg, and 1 cup of the bread crumbs to the eggplant. Taste and add the celery salt and pepper to taste. Spread the eggplant mixture in the prepared baking dish. Top with the remaining bread crumbs, and drizzle a little olive oil on top. Bake at 350 degrees about 15 minutes or until the bread crumbs are lightly browned. If using as an appetizer, serve with warm pita bread triangles or cracked pepper crackers.

—Dora Finley

CHAPTER 6

Meats and Poultry

The Streets of Heaven May Be Paved with Gold
but That Parking Lot Needs to Be
Resurfaced Before Somebody Falls and Breaks a Leg

WHEN THE SUBJECT IS MONEY

No matter how you cut it, it takes a lot of money to run a church. The building, the utilities, the various ministries, and staff salaries all come with a dollar figure attached.

The African American church has long prided itself on being a self-sufficient entity, at one time just about the only place in town where a black man (the pastor) worked for and was paid solely by other black people (the congregation).

This independence may well be one of the reasons black Protestant preachers played such a prominent role in the civil rights struggle. It was a movement organized in churches and supported by church folks. Their congregations' support allowed their pastors the freedom to be community leaders.

Times have changed, but one fact still remains—faith-based initiatives notwithstanding—the survival of churches depends on the contributions of members. This may take the form of dues, tithes, in-kind gifts, work for the church, or offerings.

In the old days, church members in some denominations were assessed specific amounts of money that they were asked to pledge as dues and pay on a predetermined schedule.

Today, tithing has generally replaced the assessment of dues. In churches that encourage tithing, all members are asked to contribute one tenth of their total income to the church. This is a biblically supported position (Malachi 3:8–10), although some church people have been known to quibble over whether the tithe should be based on their gross or their net incomes.

Offerings are gifts from church members over and above their tithes that may be designated for specific projects such as the building fund, the scholarship fund, foreign missions, or other work of the church.

In some churches, special offerings are raised, which means collected, for feeding the poor, youth programs, the church anniversary, the pastor's anniversary, or guest preachers who come to do revivals.

One-time events, such as a natural disaster or a crisis in the church family, may also generate a special offering. Fires and floods, hurricanes and tornadoes, serious illnesses, or students needing help with tuition can all elicit the astonishing generosity of church folks, and especially church ladies.

Special offerings are a topic about which nearly every church lady most surely has an opinion. Asking people to *give* is one thing. But there remain vocal pockets of believers more inclined to *raise* money for special appeals than to give out of their own pockets.

If you want to see feathers fly, bring up the subject of selling chicken dinners. No one disputes that this is a time-honored method of church fund-raising. However, in today's fast-food world, it is one that finds fewer and fewer proponents.

Food is expensive. As a result, what it takes to produce the dinners can easily wipe out any potential profit. But while preparing and selling dinners may indeed have limited utility as a fund-raising technique in the modern world, the charm of church ladies banding together to sell meals made with their own hands remains undeniable.

When everything is donated, including the food, paper products, and labor, selling dinners can actually make money. But that circumstance is increasingly rare.

There are, however, many churches with sufficient resources to sustain businesses including successful cafeterias and restaurants. And these eateries do have loyal fans who are willing to pay good money for old-fashioned, home-cooked meals. (The lure of food prepared by clean and decent church ladies who always wash their hands is undeniable.)

Other churches rely on festivals, health fairs, teas, fashion shows, concerts, bazaars, and flea markets as fund-raisers. Here and there a few churches still hold Tom Thumb weddings—events at which small children are dressed up as the bridal party and minister, and adults pledge funds in place of giving the tiny couple wedding gifts.

Church ladies make such labor-intensive

activities both fun and lucrative. These brave souls think nothing of conscripting all their friends and family to help with their projects. And they are equally comfortable bullying the local media into covering their events as they are in tapping local merchants for support.

As willing as they are to contribute to the church budget either through direct financial contributions or their lovingly staged special events, church ladies are very clear about their insistence that not a dime be wasted. Church ladies are skillful fund-raisers, but they are also frugal to the nth degree. If your church must stretch a dollar until it hollers, as the saying goes, you won't go wrong by involving church ladies in your discussions of how to do that. They are not only experts at fund-raising but also in deciding how the precious funds are spent.

Rest assured, they will allow no one to go away hungry. But they also won't spend a dime more than they must. And that, my fellow Christians, is a natural fact.

⟨⟩

Smothered Chops

Whatever happened to the plain old beef chops we enjoyed as children? I can almost taste the delicious suppers made by my grandmother starring smothered beef chops with rice and gravy, turnip greens, sliced tomatoes sprinkled with green onions, vinegar, and oil, and buttery cornbread piping hot from her oven. My beloved grandmother always made enough rice so there was plenty left over for her to transform it into a pudding for the next day's dessert. This recipe works equally well for beef, pork, or veal chops.

MAKES 3–4 SERVINGS

1 cup all-purpose flour
1 teaspoon salt
1 teaspoon pepper
1 teaspoon garlic powder
1/2 teaspoon ginger
6 pork chops
6 tablespoons vegetable oil
1 medium onion, sliced thin
3 cloves garlic, chopped fine
1 cup hot water

Mix the flour, salt, pepper, garlic powder, and ginger in a plastic bag. Put the chops in the bag and shake to coat them with the flour mixture. Remove the chops and reserve the remaining flour mixture. Heat 2 tablespoons of the oil in a cast-iron skillet, add the chops, and brown them on both sides. Remove the chops from the skillet, add 2 more tablespoons of oil, and sauté the garlic and onion until they are golden. Remove the vegetables from the skillet and add the 2 remaining tablespoons of oil. Add the flour mixture remaining in the bag and stir constantly until you have a light brown roux. Whisk in the hot water to thin the roux into a gravy. Stir in the cooked vegetables, return the chops to the gravy, reduce the heat, and cook for 20 minutes. Serve over hot cooked rice.

—Lottie Twyner Rhodes

Ce

Garlicky Stuffed Pork Roast

Whether you prepare this dish for company or for a church supper, you'll undoubtedly rack up major compliments. Be sure to remove the toothpicks before serving.

MAKES 8–10 SERVINGS

4–5 pounds boneless pork tenderloin
1 1/2 cups apple juice or apple cider
1/2 cup dried apricots, chopped fine
1/2 cup dried golden currants, white raisins, or dried cranberries
12 cloves garlic
3 cups prepared stuffing mix
2 cups peeled, cored, and finely chopped apples
1/2 teaspoon ground ginger
Salt and pepper to taste
2 teaspoons garlic powder
5 tablespoons vegetable oil

Make a deep slash along the length of the pork tenderloin to create a pocket. Warm 1/2 cup of the apple juice, add the dried apricots

and currants, and let sit until the fruits plump up; then drain. Reserve 6 of the garlic cloves in half and mince the remaining 6 cloves. With the tip of a knife, make holes in the pork tenderloin and stuff them with the sliced garlic cloves. In a bowl, combine the stuffing mix, chopped apples, plumped fruit, minced garlic, ground ginger, and the remaining 1 cup apple juice. Combine the salt, pepper, and garlic powder in a small bowl. Rub on all sides of the pork tenderloin. Preheat the oven to 350 degrees. Heat the oil in a large skillet, and brown the pork tenderloin on all sides. Remove from the heat and pack the stuffing mixture into the pocket. Close with toothpicks. Place the browned stuffed pork tenderloin in a baking dish and bake 20 minutes per pound or until the pork is done. Check for doneness by cutting a small slit in the top of the meat. Remove from the oven and let stand 10 to 15 minutes before slicing.

—Lauren Cooper

Ce

Daddy and Mommy's Barbecue

Although our concerned neighbors have called the D.C. Fire Department to our backyard more than once because of suspicious fires while I was cooking outdoors, I actually learned to barbecue from my parents who

Islands in the Storm

BRENDA RHODES MILLER
NORBECK COMMUNITY CHURCH
SILVER SPRING, MARYLAND

*Mrs. Bessie Brazley giving
Ben, Lauren, and Jay Cooper
a lesson in deportment.*

Not so many years ago, going to church was like attending a reunion for me. Toulminville-Warren United Methodist Church in Mobile, Alabama, was chock-full of relatives and close family friends.

Throughout the pews were islands of familiar faces, relatives by blood, marriage, or choice. Left and right, front and back sat people I had known and loved all my life.

Uncle Willie Eaton was the Sunday school superintendent when I was a girl. During service, his wife, my great-aunt Essie, sat beside him with two of their three sons, my cousins Harold and Al.

In the choir, my uncle Brazley sang baritone. My godmother, Joyce Irons, played the piano when the choir could manage without her lovely soprano.

My great-aunt Dot sat midway on the right side, beautifully dressed in her favorite colors, black and white. To be invited to sit with Aunt Dot was a real treat reserved for special occasions.

My own parents sat on the left-hand side, facing the pulpit, a little more than halfway back. My two sisters and I sat between our parents.

Our mother, a faithful Sunday school attendee, and our father, chair of the church administrative board, were easy to spot because of their perfect stillness. And neither one allowed any fidgeting from their children.

Aunt Bessie Ruth and Aunt Julie sometimes sat together. Other times they sat with Aunt Dot or with us.

Cousin Gussie and Cousin Randall Luke always sat near the back. My granddaddy, Wiley Bolden, sat on the left side close to the front along with his son, my uncle Ben.

My godfather, John Irons, was usually in front of us with his four children. He and Daddy sometimes tiptoed out of church to talk in the parking lot when service ran long.

My dear friend Mrs. Hughes sat three rows from the front on the right side along with Mrs. Woods. Both were communion stewards and Sunday school teachers.

Left and right, front, back, and center, relatives and family friends filled the church. They were not the *entire* congregation, but their presence was significant. Seeing all of them each Sunday gave me a sense of security and stability regardless of what the outside world might hold.

Several months ago I attended church with Daddy. Looking around, I nearly sobbed. It was painfully obvious who was gone. Aunt Essie and Uncle Willie. Cousin Al. Granddaddy. Uncle Ben. Aunt Dot and Uncle Brazley. Cousin Gussie and Cousin Randall. Mamma. Mrs. Hughes and Mrs. Woods.

Just a few months later, Daddy was gone too.

never suffered similar indignities in Mobile, Alabama.

MAKES 8 SERVINGS

3 cups apple cider vinegar
2 tablespoons "liquid smoke"
1 tablespoon garlic powder
1 cup vegetable oil
4 racks pork ribs or 4 whole chickens cut in
quarters
4 cups prepared barbecue sauce plus
additional for serving

Combine the vinegar, liquid smoke, garlic powder, and oil in a baking pan large enough to hold the meat in a single layer, add the ribs or chicken, and marinate in the refrigerator overnight, turning at least three times. Re-move the meat and discard the marinade. Place the ribs or chicken on a hot grill and cook until brown on both sides, turning frequently to avoid burning. Preheat the oven to 300 degrees.

Place the browned ribs or chicken in a baking dish, cover them with the barbecue sauce, and bake until all the sauce is absorbed. Serve with extra sauce on the side.

—*Charles Rhodes and Lolita Bolden Rhodes*

Easy Barbecued Country Spare Ribs

Country spare ribs are just chops disguised as big hunks of pork. They're often on sale and whatever the season, they make a delicious and low-cost main course.

MAKES 8–10 SERVINGS

6 cloves garlic
8 pounds country spare ribs
Salt and pepper to taste

Vegetable oil cooking spray
1 (18-ounce) bottle prepared
    barbecue sauce

Bring 4 quarts of water to a boil in a large stockpot. Add the garlic cloves and the ribs and boil for 10 minutes. Remove the ribs from the water and season them on all sides with salt and pepper. Preheat the oven to 400 degrees. Place a large baking sheet in the oven until the sheet is hot. Spray the ribs with the cooking spray, place them on the hot baking sheet, and cook until brown. Pour the barbecue sauce in a large bowl. Dip the hot ribs in

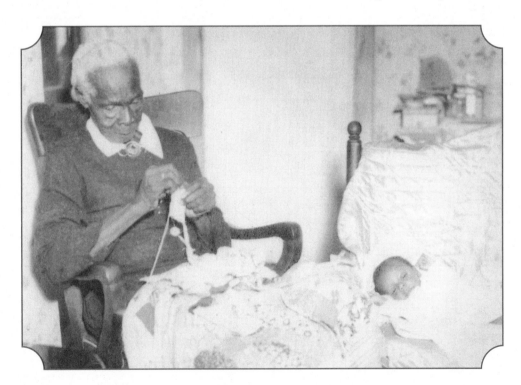

Mrs. Charlotte Hannon sews a patchwork quilt in El Campo, Texas, circa 1950.
She was Rev. Courtenay L. Miller's great great grandmother.

sauce and return them to the baking sheet. Increase the oven temperature to 425 degrees and bake the ribs until the sauce is sizzling. Remove from oven and serve with potato salad and baked beans for a picnic supper or with mashed potatoes and a vegetable for a delicious evening meal composed of old-fashioned comfort food.

—*Courtenay L. Miller*

Ce

Baked Trotters

Trotters are simply pigs' feet. Although few church ladies will admit to cooking them, they do turn up fairly often at church suppers. When baked with the skin removed, the meat is tender and flavorful. When cooked in their skins, trotters can turn into a gelatinous mass that looks unappetizing but tastes good. There are partisans for both methods. And for those squeamish souls who won't try pigs' feet at all, ham hocks work just as well with this recipe.

MAKES 4–6 SERVINGS

3 pounds pigs feet
4 cloves garlic, crushed
Salt and pepper to taste
2 large onions, sliced thin
1 (16-ounce) jar prepared barbecue sauce or
prepared pasta sauce of your choice.

Dip each foot into boiling water for 2 to 3 minutes. Remove from the water and scrape off any hairs. Place the cleaned pigs' feet in a Dutch oven and add cool water to cover. Add ½ teaspoon of salt and the crushed garlic. Bring the water to a boil and cook the trotters until the meat separates from the bone. Remove them with a slotted spoon and pull the meat away from the skin. Preheat the oven to 400 degrees. Layer the meat and the sliced onions in a baking dish and season with pepper. Cover with the barbecue sauce and bake 15 to 20 minutes. Try serving these with baked beans and cole slaw.

Ce

Dinner Ham Slice

Every now and then you may have a taste for ham but don't feel like going to the trouble of baking one. In that case, buy a slice or two and prepare it this way for a fast and easy dinner dish.

MAKES 4 SERVINGS

2 slices ham, about 1 inch thick
⅓ cup brown sugar
2 Granny Smith apples, sliced thin
4 tablespoons (½ stick) butter

Preheat the oven to 400 degrees. Put the ham slices in a shallow baking dish and sprinkle them with half the brown sugar. Spread two layers of apple over the ham, sprinkle with the remaining brown sugar, and dot with the butter. Cover the pan with foil, and bake 40 minutes. Uncover and brown for 10 minutes longer.

—*Adapted from* The Household Searchlight Recipe Book

Ce

Perfect Prime Rib

Maybe you don't want to eat beef every day, but when you do want it, try this satisfying recipe.

MAKES 8–10 SERVINGS

1 (5-pound) rib roast of beef
10 cloves garlic, peeled and sliced
10–12 fresh thyme sprigs
4 tablespoons adobo seasoning
2 tablespoons garlic powder
Canola oil, as needed

Preheat the oven to 500 degrees. Rinse the roast and wipe it dry. Poke holes all over the surface of the roast and insert slivers of garlic. Score the fat and insert the thyme sprigs. Mix the adobo seasoning with the garlic powder and enough oil to make a paste. Rub the paste over the entire surface of the roast.

Heat the roasting pan in the oven and, when it is hot, place the roast fat side down in the pan and return it to the oven. Cook 15 minutes and turn the roast fat side up.

Reduce the oven temperature to 325 degrees, and cook for about 1 hour and 15 minutes. Remove the roast from the oven and let it sit for 10 minutes before slicing. The first few slices should be well done and the rest will be medium well or medium.

—*Brenda Rhodes Miller*

Ce

Luscious Liver

You say you hate liver? That's probably because you've only eaten it cooked until it was as tough as shoe leather. This recipe might well change your mind. Even plain old beef liver, which costs much less than calves' liver, tastes delicious cooked this way.

MAKES 6 SERVINGS

2 pounds sliced beef liver
Salt and pepper to taste
1 cup buttermilk
½ pound thick-sliced bacon
2 large onions, thinly sliced
2–4 tablespoons vegetable oil, as needed
4 tablespoons all-purpose flour, seasoned with salt and pepper
¼ cup capers with their liquid

Rinse the liver, pulling off any stringy parts. Using the edge of a saucer, pound the liver until it is thin. This will break down the fibers so the liver cooks more quickly. Pat the liver dry and season both sides with salt and pepper. Let the liver stand for 5 minutes. Put the liver in a plastic bag that seals. Pour in the buttermilk and seal the bag.

Turn the bag frequently, letting the liver sit in the buttermilk, in the refrigerator, for at least 1 hour. Cook the bacon in a large skillet until it is done but not crisp. Remove from the pan and set it aside to drain on paper towels. Sauté the onions in the bacon grease along with the 2 tablespoons of the oil. Remove the onions when they are golden and set the skillet aside. Remove the liver from the bag and shake off any liquid. Lightly pat the seasoned flour on both sides of liver. Quickly brown the liver on both sides in the skillet in which you cooked the bacon and onions, adding more oil if necessary, and being careful not to overcook it. Remove the liver and return the bacon and onions to the pan. Cook for 5 minutes. Pour the capers with their liquid into the pan and cook 1 minute longer. Remove the pan from the heat and top each slice of liver with onions, bacon, and capers.

Serve with mashed potatoes and a vegetable.

—*Brenda Rhodes Miller*

Mama's Pepper Steak

Even the most inexpensive cuts of beef can make delicious meals. Use round or chuck steak for this dish.

MAKES 6 SERVINGS

2 pounds boneless round or chuck steak
Salt and pepper to taste
4 tablespoons all-purpose flour
2 green or red bell peppers, seeded and sliced
*   in strips*
¼ cup vegetable oil

Pound the steak thin with a mallet or the side of a saucer. Salt and pepper both sides of the steak, then slice the meat into 2-inch-wide strips. Dredge the strips in the flour and set aside. Sauté the bell peppers in 2 tablespoons of the oil until wilted. Remove the peppers from the pan and brown the steak on all sides in the remaining 2 tablespoons of oil. Return the pepper strips to the pan and cook with the steak for 10 minutes more. Serve with a starch and vegetable.

—*Carolyn Lolita Bolden Rhodes*

Never Too Early or Too Late to Call

JOHNNIE OVERTON
PARKWAY GARDENS PRESBYTERIAN CHURCH
MEMPHIS, TENNESSEE

Most people as busy as Johnnie Overton would try to keep office hours. But she puts no time limit on her Christian service.

"People know they can come to me any time they want something done. I'll follow through on what I'm asked to accomplish. I enjoy being busy."

Mrs. Overton is a member of the Chancel Choir and Witness Committee as well as an elder and a deacon on rotation. Active with the Presbyterian Women, specifically the Flower Circle, she has served as secretary, treasurer, vice moderator, moderator, and Circle leader. She studies in the church's Covenant Life Sunday school class. She steps forward when her church participates in the Memphis Interfaith Hospitality Network, providing shelter and food for homeless families.

Immediate past corresponding secretary and member of the Greater Area Memphis Chapter of the National Black Presbyterian Caucus, Mrs. Overton has served as a tutor in an after-school program sponsored by her church and the Caucus.

She especially enjoys singing with the Chancel Choir, which provides the music for the 11 A.M. service. "I've always loved to sing, but I don't have a great voice. I can carry a tune. But don't ask me to do a solo. If I do, it will be so low you won't be able to hear me," she explains with a laugh.

But Mrs. Overton doesn't hesitate to speak her mind to put new ideas in place. Doing such work in the church is not all sunshine and roses.

"You won't always have the majority with you. There are times when you must stand alone," she says. "I always told my children that and it's true."

People don't park their personalities at the church door, and Mrs. Overton cautions that it is important to handle difficult people with care.

"Love conquers hate. Where you have any discord, if you continue to exhibit a positive attitude and act with love, you will win them over."

Spoken like a true church lady.

Flank Steak

The secret to flank steak is to slice it against the grain. While the ingredients in this recipe may sound like a strange combination, they actually work quite well together.

MAKES 8–10 SERVINGS

2 pounds flank steak
1½ cups ketchup
1 (6-ounce) package of French onion soup
    mix
Cooking oil

Preheat the oven to 400 degrees. Wipe the flank steak and remove any bits of fat. Spread the steak with a layer of ketchup. Shake the soup mix and sprinkle it over the ketchup. Roll the flank steak into a log and secure it with skewers. Heat the cooking oil in a large heavy skillet, and brown the log on all sides. Transfer it to a baking pan and bake about 30 minutes or until the steak is done to your liking. Slice against the grain and serve.

—Rena Simmons

Beef with Sugar Snap Peas

Almost every grocery store and supermarket offers a wide variety of exotic vegetables fresh, frozen, and canned. This recipe calls for sugar snap peas, fresh ginger, green onions, bean sprouts, and mushrooms.

MAKES 6–8 SERVINGS

½ cup all-purpose flour
Salt and pepper to taste
2 pounds flank steak, sliced against the grain
1 cup sesame oil
1 pound mushrooms, sliced
3–4 green onions, chopped
1 pound angel hair pasta
1 cup soy sauce
¼ cup rice wine vinegar
⅓ cup packed light brown sugar
1 teaspoon grated fresh ginger
1 tablespoon cornstarch
1 cup bean sprouts
1 pound sugar snap peas
¼ cup sesame seeds, toasted

Combine the flour with the salt and pepper in a plastic bag. Shake the sliced flank steak in the flour mixture. Heat ⅓ cup of the sesame oil in a large skillet and brown the meat on all sides. Set the meat aside, add another ⅓ cup of oil to the skillet, and sauté the mushrooms and green onions until tender. Remove the pan from the heat. Cook the pasta in a large pot of boiling water until just tender. Drain and set it aside. In a small pot, heat the soy sauce, rice wine vinegar, brown sugar, and grated ginger. Simmer for 8 minutes. Whisk ¼ cup of the hot soy sauce mixture into the cornstarch, then stir the heated cornstarch into the remaining soy sauce mixture. Return the meat to the skillet with the mushrooms and green onions, add the bean sprouts, snap peas, and the remaining ⅓ cup of oil. Toss and cook until the snap peas and bean sprouts are done. Add the soy sauce mixture and cook another 3 to 4 minutes. Arrange the pasta on a platter and top with the meat mixture. Toss well, sprinkle with the toasted sesame seeds, and serve.

Note: You can serve the beef and peas over rice instead of pasta if you prefer.

—Joyce Clemons

Ce

Pastor's in Trouble Meat Loaf

A certain young pastor once mentioned from his pulpit that "every now and then a man wants meat loaf." His wife, who fancied herself a gourmet cook, had never ever deigned to prepare such a mundane dish for him, but in response to his sermon, she promptly cooked up a delicious meat loaf the size of Texas, which he had to eat every day for nearly two weeks. And now, whenever he comes home to find meat loaf for dinner, he asks in bewilderment, "Honey, what did I do wrong this time?"

MAKES 6–8 SERVINGS

2 pounds ground round
1 pound ground pork
3 large eggs, beaten
2 tablespoons chopped fresh rosemary
2 tablespoons sage
2 tablespoons thyme
¼ cup chopped fresh flat-leaf parsley
1 cup Italian bread crumbs
Salt and freshly ground pepper to taste,
    if desired
1 (3-ounce) can tomato paste
¼ cup cane sugar syrup

Preheat the oven to 400 degrees. Grease a 9-by-5-inch loaf pan. Lightly combine the first 8 ingredients on the list. Season with salt and pepper, if desired. Spoon the mixture into the greased loaf pan and bake for 40 minutes or until the meat loaf is browned. Combine the tomato paste and cane syrup in a small bowl. Spoon it over the meat and bake an additional 10 to 15 minutes. Serve with garlic mashed potatoes and a vegetable.

—Brenda Rhodes Miller

Ce

Speaking the Truth in Love

ADAH E. PIERCE
ASPEN HILL CHRISTIAN CHURCH
SILVER SPRING, MARYLAND

Wherever she goes, Adah E. Pierce is committed to fostering good communication. She learned this valuable lesson from her parents, especially her mother.

Mrs. Pierce joined the church at the age of twelve in Hawkins, Texas, home of Jarvis Christian College. Even before professing her faith, however, she was involved in activities built around people talking to one another in respectful and supportive ways.

Her mother, Arzelia Mae Jones Edwards, was a lay pastor and an accomplished musician who wrote both words and lyrics for the school songs of Hawkins Colored High School and Jarvis Christian College.

"My mother was a strong instrument of faith upon me," says Mrs. Pierce. "She instilled a lot of community and self-pride in young people."

One of the ways Mrs. Edwards did this was to launch a Progressive Intercultural Club that guided young people in social, moral, spiritual, and cultural development. The group met weekly in the Edwards home for discussions, study, and prayer.

Her only requirement was that students must live a morally fit and respectable life and she frequently quoted her daughter's high school creed to underscore the point.

> I have to live with myself, and so
> I want to be fit for myself to know.
> I want to be able, as the days go by,
> Always to look myself straight in the eye.
> I don't want to stand with the setting sun
> And hate myself for the things I've done.

The lessons Adah Pierce learned from her mother carried over to her choice of career. A social worker by training, she now counsels teens and young adults. She is also deeply involved in helping troubled marriages survive by working with couples from a spiritual perspective.

Mrs. Pierce constantly stresses the importance of healthy communication. Her actions demonstrate that speaking the truth in love can heal the soul.

Gosh, It's Goulash

Goulash is just plain old stew with an accent. If veal isn't on sale, go ahead and use beef. Don't buy costly stewing beef though; just buy chuck or round steak and cut it up yourself. This is the perfect dish to take to a wintertime church supper.

MAKES 4–6 SERVINGS

1 cup diced salt pork or bacon fat
1/2 cup diced celery
1 cup diced green or red bell pepper
1/2 cup chopped onion
2 pounds cubed beef or veal
Salt and pepper to taste
2 tablespoons all-purpose flour
4 cups beef stock
2 cups stewed tomatoes
1 3/4 cups chopped carrots
1/2 cup chopped green onions
1/4 cup minced fresh flat-leaf parsley
3 teaspoons allspice
3 cloves
3 cups egg noodles

Cook the salt pork in a Dutch oven to release the fat. Sauté the celery, bell pepper, and onion in the fat from the salt pork. Season the beef cubes with salt and pepper and roll them in the flour. Add to the Dutch oven and brown on all sides. When the meat has browned, add the stock to the pan and cook until the meat is tender. Add the remaining vegetables and spices and, if necessary, enough water to keep all the ingredients covered. Reduce the heat and cook 20 to 30 minutes or until the vegetables are soft. Prepare the noodles according to the package directions. Serve the goulash over noodles.

Note: For a thicker goulash, stir 2 tablespoons cornstarch into the broth during the last 10 minutes of cooking.

—*Adapted from* The Household Searchlight Recipe Book

Champion's Chili

There's no law mandating having chili at church Fall Festivals and Men's Ministry Football Dinners, but for some reason autumn and chili just seem to go well together.

MAKES 8 SERVINGS

1 pound ground beef
1 pound ground pork
1 large onion, sliced thin
1 large green bell pepper, diced
5 cloves garlic, chopped
1 (6-ounce) can tomato paste
1 (1.8-ounce) package chili mix
1 (14-ounce) can black beans, drained
1 (14-ounce) can corn, drained
2 cups water
1 tablespoon cumin
1/4 cup chopped fresh cilantro
Salt and pepper, to taste
1/4 cup fine cornmeal
4 cups cooked white rice

Brown the ground beef and ground pork in a large stockpot. Add the vegetables and cook until soft. Add the tomato paste and chili mix. Stir well and continue to cook for 5 minutes. Pour in the canned beans and canned corn. Add the cumin and cilantro. Cook for 5 minutes. Taste, and add salt and pepper if needed. Stir in the cornmeal and simmer the chili for 20 minutes, stirring often. Serve over the rice.

—Leslie Williams

Ce

Leg of Lamb

Can you imagine? There are actually people who never eat lamb! Poor things. They've never had the pleasure of enjoying tender, mild-flavored lamb cooked with garden herbs and spices. Serve them a leg of lamb roasted this way and you are sure to change their minds.

MAKES 10–12 SERVINGS

1 (5- to 6-pound) leg of lamb
5 large cloves garlic, peeled and sliced
5 sprigs fresh rosemary
1 cup unflavored yogurt
½ cup chopped fresh garlic
2 teaspoons ground cinnamon
2 teaspoons ground cardamom
¼ cup grated fresh ginger
1 tablespoon brown sugar

1½ teaspoons salt
1½ teaspoons pepper

Preheat the oven to 450 degrees. With a sharp knife, remove the layer of thick white fat (called the "fell") covering the leg of lamb. Wash the leg of lamb and pat it dry. Using a sharp knife, make deep slits in the surface of the meat and insert slices of garlic and sprigs of rosemary throughout. In a bowl, combine the yogurt, chopped garlic, cinnamon, cardamom, ginger, brown sugar, salt, and pepper. Heat a roasting pan with a rack in the oven. Cover the leg of lamb with the yogurt mixture, and place it on the heated rack. After 15 minutes, reduce the oven temperature to 350 degrees and cook the lamb until the yogurt coating is golden brown or lamb registers 175 degrees, for medium, on an instant-read meat thermometer.

—Brenda Rhodes Miller

Ce

Lamb Stew

Once you cook a leg of lamb, unless your family eats like mine does, you can expect to get several meals from it. Lamb stew is a great way to use leftover lamb and vegetables, and I bet this recipe will be your all-time favorite.

MAKES 4 SERVINGS

¼ cup cooking oil
1 cup chopped celery
2 cloves garlic, chopped
1 cup chopped onions
3 tablespoons all-purpose flour
Salt and pepper to taste
1 (16-ounce) can beef or vegetable broth
1 tablespoon summer savory or tarragon
2½ cups cooked lamb cubes
1 cup diced parsnips
1 cup chopped carrots
1 cup peeled and cubed raw potatoes
2 cups cooked mashed potatoes or rice

In a Dutch oven, heat the oil, and sauté the celery, garlic, and onions. Stir in the flour and cook until browned. Taste, and add salt and pepper as needed. Whisk in the broth until smooth. Add the summer savory and all the remaining ingredients except the mashed potatoes or rice. Stir and add water to cover. Reduce the heat, cover, and cook on low, adding water as needed, until vegetables are tender. Taste and adjust the seasoning, adding more summer savory, salt, and pepper as needed. Serve the stew in bowls with a scoop of mashed potatoes or rice in the center.

—Millicent Bolden

Whole Gingered Chicken on a Can

Chicken is such a versatile meat that it can be successfully combined with a wide variety of ingredients. Whole chickens are almost always less expensive than chicken parts, and this recipe lets the whole chicken shine.

MAKES 6–8 SERVINGS

1 (3-pound) roasting chicken
1 cup ginger marmalade
1 (12-ounce) can ginger beer or ginger ale
2 lemons
8 tablespoons (½ cup) butter, melted

Preheat the oven to 500 degrees. Wash and clean the roasting chicken and pat it dry.

Combine the ginger marmalade with half the ginger beer, the juice of one lemon, and the melted butter. Rub the chicken inside and out with the marmalade mixture. Cut the remaining lemon into three pieces and stuff them into the cavity of the chicken. Set the remaining ½ can of ginger beer in a roasting pan and stand the chicken vertically on the can. Place chicken, standing up on the can in the oven for 15 minutes. Reduce the oven temperature to 350 degrees, and cook the chicken for 30 to 45 minutes or until the skin is golden and the juices run clear when pierced with a fork.

—Dora Finley

Chicken and Ham Rolls

My brother-in-law shared this recipe with me long ago and far away. I've made a few changes over the years that I hope haven't hurt his dish too much.

MAKES 8 SERVINGS

8 boneless, skinless chicken breasts
8 slices salty ham
8 slices mozzarella cheese
8 large basil leaves
1 cup freshly grated Parmesan cheese
1/2 cup plus 3 tablespoons olive oil
1 pound angel hair pasta
1 pound fresh spinach leaves, well washed
   and blanched
1 pound fresh ripe tomatoes, sliced
Salt and pepper to taste

Preheat the oven to 350 degrees. Place the chicken breasts between sheets of plastic wrap and pound them thin with a mallet or the edge of a saucer. Lay a slice of ham, then a slice of cheese and a basil leaf on each pounded breast. Sprinkle with half the Parmesan cheese, roll up the breasts, and secure the rolls with toothpicks. Brown the breasts in the ½ cup olive oil, then transfer them to a 9-by-13-inch baking dish and bake 20 minutes. Cook the pasta in a large pot of boiling water. When done, drain and toss with the remaining 3 tablespoons of oil. Arrange spinach leaves on a platter. Top with the pasta and season with salt and pepper to taste. Arrange the chicken over the pasta, garnish with the tomato slices, and sprinkle with the remaining Parmesan cheese.

—Brenda Rhodes Miller

Perfect Fried Chicken

Perfectly seasoned fried chicken is something every church supper requires. Rena Simmons not only prepared her exceptional fried chicken for me, she also graciously shared her recipe.

MAKES 6–8 SERVINGS

4 pounds chicken pieces
1 tablespoon Old Bay seasoning
2 teaspoons lemon/herb seasoning
1 tablespoon Original Fried Chicken
   Seasoning
2 teaspoons garlic powder
1 teaspoon garlic pepper
Salt to taste
3 cups all-purpose flour
1 quart peanut or canola oil

Place the chicken pieces in a colander and rinse them under cold running water. Allow the chicken to drain but do not dry it. In a small bowl, combine the seasonings, garlic powder, garlic pepper, and salt. Lay the chicken pieces on waxed paper and sprinkle half the seasoning mixture over them. Combine the flour and the remaining half of the seasoning mixture in a brown paper bag. Add the chicken and shake to coat it well. Fill a cast-iron skillet half full of oil. Heat on high. To test if it's hot enough, sprinkle a few drops of water into the oil; if it sizzles, the oil has reached the proper temperature. Gently place chicken in the hot oil, reduce the heat to medium, cover, and cook for approximately 10 minutes. Uncover and turn the chicken to cook on the other side. Continue turning the chicken pieces until browned on all sides. Pierce the chicken parts with a fork. If the juices run clear, the chicken is done. If the juices are pink, continue frying until the juices are clear. When the chicken is browned and fully done, remove from skillet and drain on a brown paper bag covered with paper towels.

Note: Never cover fried chicken with foil, plastic wrap, or waxed paper. Always cover with a cloth towel to keep the chicken crisp.

—Rena Simmons

Southern Fried Chicken Marinated in Hot Sauce

Some people swear by Crystal Hot Sauce; others are fans of Tabasco or Texas Pete. Whatever your preference, it is the hot sauce marinade that makes this fried chicken super-delicious.

Just be sure you don't leave the chicken parts in the marinade for more than a few hours. Overnight will make it too hot and spicy!

MAKES 10 SERVINGS

6 pounds chicken parts
2 cups hot sauce
6 cups vegetable oil
2 cups all-purpose flour
1/4 tablespoon seasoned salt
1 teaspoon black pepper
1 teaspoon lemon-pepper salt
Scant 1/2 teaspoon monosodium glutamate
   (optional)

Wash the chicken parts, and pat them dry. Place the chicken in a large bowl and cover it with the hot sauce. Refrigerate and let the chicken marinate in the hot sauce for several hours, shaking the bowl frequently to be sure all the parts are covered in sauce. When you are ready to cook, heat the oil in a large cast-iron skillet. Combine the flour, salts, pepper, and monosodium glutamate, if using it, in a brown paper bag. Remove the chicken from the hot sauce and shake it in the flour mixture. Brown the chicken on all sides in the hot oil. When the chicken has browned, reduce the heat, cover the skillet, and fry until the chicken is cooked through. Don't overcrowd the pan. Cook the chicken in batches if necessary. Drain on newspaper covered with paper towels.

—Brenda Rhodes Miller

Joy Today Is Mine

JOYCE McCANNON
ATONEMENT EPISCOPAL CHURCH
WASHINGTON, D.C.

The exquisite vestments worn by the Episcopal priest, the chalice used for Communion, the baptismal font, the pristine altar cloths, even the candles illuminating the service don't get there by magic. It is no accident when an altar is perfectly set. Church linens are not wash-and-wear. Sacramental items require high maintenance. That is the job of the Altar Guild.

Joyce McCannon is a member of the Altar Guild at Atonement Episcopal Church in Washington, D.C. Her guild is made up of several teams of three to five church ladies.

An entire manual guides the work of the Guild. The manual clearly states what must be done and how to do it. Guild members launder, press, and arrange the altar cloths. Each cloth has a distinct folding pattern that guild members must learn along with the cloths' names.

All the cloths on the altar are called fair linen. The largest one, laid down for Communion, is the corporal. The square of linen covering the cup is the Communion veil. When the priest washes his hands before Communion, he dries his hands on the lavabo towel. The cloth used to wipe the Communion cup is the purificator.

Every week, these church ladies dust the wood and marble of the altar. They wash and iron linens and vestments, polish the brass or silver as well as arrange the flowers. Gone are the days when beeswax candles lit the altar. Now guild members have mastered the technique of filling newfangled candle sleeves with liquid.

To stay on their toes, Altar Guild members meet every couple of months to problem solve and to hear news of their diocese. Each region convenes its Altar Guilds annually for a workshop during which members pray, network, and attend to any changes in the Liturgy.

Joyce McCannon sees being an Altar Guild member as a sacred charge. Without the work of the Altar Guild, the actual services would not take place. She says the guild does its work when no one is looking, and members seek no credit. Joining the Altar Guild means being willing to get your hands dirty. Members work hard, rejoicing all the while.

Chicken-Fried Steak

Hardly anyone seems to make chicken-fried steak anymore, but when you do, remember to pound in the flour. Pounding tenderizes the meat and the flour gives the beef its chicken-fried texture.

MAKES 2 SERVINGS

Salt and pepper to taste
1 pound round steak, no more than ¾ inch
*   thick*
1 cup all-purpose flour
¼ teaspoon garlic salt
¼ teaspoon cayenne pepper
1 large egg, lightly beaten
¼ cup cooking oil, or more as needed
Milk or water

Rub the salt and pepper into both sides of the steak. Combine the flour with the garlic salt and cayenne pepper. With a meat mallet or the edge of a saucer, pound half the flour mixture into both sides of the steak. Then dip the steak in the beaten egg and dredge it in the remaining flour. Heat the cooking oil in a large, heavy skillet. Add the steak and fry until brown on one side; turn the steak and brown the other side, adding more oil if necessary. Reduce the heat and continue cooking until meat is done. Remove the steak and pour off any fat remaining in the skillet. Add just enough milk or water to the skillet to scrape up the browned bits and make a gravy.

Season to taste and serve the gravy over the steak.

—*Adapted from* The Household Searchlight
    Recipe Book

Party Chicken Breasts

Canned tomatoes now come flavored with hot peppers, Italian seasoning, and many other tasty additions. These variations make it easy to prepare a festive dish using little more than ordinary chicken breasts. The Italian tomatoes in this recipe, for example, come flavored with basil and oregano.

MAKES 6–8 SERVINGS

6–8 boneless, skinless chicken breasts
Salt and pepper to taste
5 tablespoons olive oil
1 (14.5-ounce) can diced Italian tomatoes,
*   with their liquid*
1 cup seasoned bread crumbs

Preheat the oven to 400 degrees. Season the chicken breasts with salt and pepper. Heat the olive oil in a large skillet and brown the chicken on both sides. Pour a layer of diced tomatoes on the bottom of a 9-by-13-inch baking dish and add the chicken breasts.

Cover with the remaining diced tomatoes,

Making Room For God

MRS. MARTHA CHUBB
MONTVALE FIRST BAPTIST CHURCH
MONTVALE, VIRGINIA

Mrs. Martha Chubb is a poised church lady of medium height whose erect posture belies her years. Always impeccably dressed, she brings a commonsense approach to religion.

"Why do you think they break the cracker into pieces for Communion?" she asks. "Because no one can swallow it whole," is her answer.

That seems on its face to be a simple statement of fact, and the charming Mrs. Chubb knows how to use such simple examples to illustrate the challenges of faith.

"God breaks us before we can serve. Whatever God has for us to do, we have to be broken to make room for it. He wants us to be humble and well prepared so we can do His ministry."

Mrs. Chubb believes that when church ladies minister, they must do so in love with a spirit of humility.

"Know God for yourself," she admonishes. "Know what He is saying to *you*. Get some quiet in your life so you can hear what He wants you to do. Push that self out of the way so He has room to come into your life."

According to Mrs. Chubb, it is especially important for women of faith to allow God rather than man to lead them. And if that means taking a backseat rather than seeking the limelight, so be it. Her advice is to follow God wherever He leads.

No matter what tradition, custom, or someone else might have to say, women must always follow God, she advises. And, bowing her head in acceptance of God's great plan, she says, "I'd rather be back in the kitchen wearing my apron than up in the front wearing a fancy hat."

top with the seasoned bread crumbs, and bake about 20 minutes.

—Millicent Bolden

Ce

Make-It-Last-Forever Chicken

Whole boneless, skinless chicken breasts are usually quite thick. In order to feed more people with the same amount of chicken, slice each breast into several thin filets. The chicken will cook quickly and absorb the flavor of the seasonings.

MAKES 6–8 SERVINGS

4 whole boneless, skinless chicken breasts, sliced thin horizontally
Salt and pepper to taste
¼ cup dried oregano
½ cup olive oil
2 pounds fresh baby spinach, washed well
Juice of 1 lemon
¼ cup shredded fresh basil leaves
¼ pound prosciutto, cut into 1-inch dice

Season both sides of the chicken breast slices with salt and pepper. Pat them with the oregano. Heat ¼ cup of the olive oil in a large skillet, add the chicken, and cook, turning once or twice, until done. Do not overcook. Remove the chicken from the skillet and arrange it in a circle on a platter with the slices overlapping. Add the remaining olive oil to the skillet along with spinach and cook just until wilted. Season the spinach with salt and pepper and mound it in the center of the platter. Add the lemon juice to the skillet, and stir to make a light sauce. Pour the sauce over chicken slices. Serve sprinkled with the shredded basil and diced proscuitto.

—Camille S. Hall

Fish and Seafood

There Are No Pockets in a Shroud

HOW CHURCH LADIES CONFRONT MORTALITY

*F*or women of faith, life on earth, with all its struggles, is but a short stop on the journey to heaven. Church ladies strive to use each day as if it were the first and last day they will ever see.

For them, every opportunity to help someone else is a blessing from God. They believe in thanking God for every challenge they encounter. Prayer is a constant source of strength, and as a result, they pray without ceasing.

Their belief in eternal life fuels their good works and gives them the courage to face whatever life might bring. While church ladies may live in the here and now, they keep their eyes forever fixed on the hereafter.

My grandmother, Lottie Twyner Rhodes, was a church lady of the first order. She belonged to Samuel Chapel AME Church in Prichard, Alabama, where the doors rarely opened without her being present. She was an usher, a Communion steward, and a faithful member of the pew through thick and thin.

Grandmother was also an amazingly generous woman. She believed in giving both time and money not only to her church but also to less fortunate members of the community. The annual Country Fair to which she contributed patchwork quilts, velvet pillows, and homemade preserves was held to raise funds for Samuel Chapel. The items she contributed were always best-sellers, but she also arranged for other women of the church to provide their own special items.

Dolls wearing lacy crocheted dresses to cover rolls of toilet tissue, holiday wreaths of pine cones and fragrant herbs crowned with bright red ribbons, Christmas trees made of old telephone books gaily decorated with tiny ornaments, jars of vinegar flavored with hot peppers, along with pickles and jellies made with garden produce were but a few of the things other church ladies made for the fair.

And when it came to money, Grandmother had what seemed like an endless supply of coins, which she kept in Mason jars under her bed and distributed freely to her grandchildren as rewards for good grades in school, particularly those that recognized exceptionally good behavior.

Sometimes, for no reason at all, she showered us with her largesse of coins, always encouraging us to save a portion of whatever she gave us—which we did.

I have no doubt that many other people also benefited from her generosity, for our grandmother was well known as a woman who gave without counting the cost.

From time to time, one of Grandmother's grown children, either an aunt or my father, might have hinted that her generosity would all too soon deplete her resources. But Grandmother always had a ready comeback. "There are no pockets in a shroud," she would say with an indulgent smile.

When I was a little girl, I had no idea what a shroud was. I hadn't learned to read yet, so I couldn't look up the word in the dictionary, which is what Grandmother always told my older cousin to do when she had a question about a word she didn't understand. So I asked Grandmother to explain shroud to me.

"A shroud is what dead people wear," she said. "It is a long, loose gown."

"What does it mean when you say it doesn't have any pockets?"

"All it means is that people ought to give everything they can while they are alive and able to help."

Over the years, I've heard other church ladies echo Grandmother's wisdom. They understand that life is fleeting, and no one knows the day or the hour when it will end. While that may strike fear into the hearts of many people, it does not seem to intimidate church ladies one bit.

Their belief in the Resurrection is what gives them the courage to keep trying every day and in every way to love God and love their neighbors. It is an active, visible love that paves their path to life everlasting.

I thank my grandmother for allowing me to watch her walk that path.

Pan-Fried Fish with Lemon

Any firm-fleshed white fish, whether whiting, haddock, or catfish, tastes great in this preparation. Equally tasty at breakfast, lunch, or dinner, the fish should be served with a starch so the delicious pan juices are not wasted.

MAKES 6 SERVINGS

6 fish fillets
1/2 cup hot sauce
5 tablespoons olive oil
Juice of 1/2 lemon

Marinate the fish fillets for 10 to 15 minutes in the hot sauce. Heat the olive oil in a large skillet. Place the fish fillets in the skillet and cook, covered, until the fish flakes when tested with a fork. Remove the fish from the skillet, add the lemon juice to the pan drippings, and cook for 3 minutes. Serve the fish with grits or mashed potatoes topped with the sauce from the skillet.

—Camille Samples

Fish in Foil

Tired of fried or baked fish? Try this effortless way of preparing fresh or frozen boneless, skin-less fish fillets. The recipe is so easy you may want to make a batch for the next potluck supper at church.

MAKES 4–6 SERVINGS

1/4 cup butter
4–6 boneless, skinless fish fillets of your
    choice
Salt and pepper to taste
1 cup thinly sliced onions
1 cup shredded carrots
1 cup thinly sliced red or yellow bell peppers
1/2 cup fresh thyme leaves
1 lemon, sliced thin
4–6 tablespoons olive oil

Preheat the oven to 400 degrees. Tear off sheets of aluminum foil large enough to hold one fillet apiece. Grease the foil with the butter. Season both sides of the fillets with salt and pepper. Top each one with a portion of the vegetables, herbs, several lemon slices, and 1 tablespoon olive oil. Fold the top of the foil and then crimp the sides, making an envelope and leaving a little room for expansion. Place the foil packets on a cookie sheet, and bake for 15 minutes. Remove from the oven and let stand for 5 minutes. Serve one fillet per person.

—Lauren Cooper

Lord Prepare Me to be a Sanctuary,
Pure and Holy, Tried and True

A Church Lady Who Prefers to Remain Nameless

A certain church lady, who prefers to remain nameless, was a fan of revivals when she was a young girl.

Tent revivals were outdoor worship services. The rallying cry of such revivals was, "Whosoever will, let them come." In her little country town, they were the highlight of the summer.

People started arriving in the cool of the evening, settling themselves into wooden folding chairs to enjoy several hours of testifying, singing, and preaching. The local funeral home passed out cardboard fans for the comfort of the worshippers.

As a child, our nameless church lady was an avid worshipper who delighted in the dramatic preaching style practiced by visiting revivalists.

"They weren't hellfire and brimstone preachers who tried to scare people to Salvation. These were men who talked about the goodness of God and His unending mercies," she remembers.

Any tent revival worth its salt measured its success in the number of souls brought to Christ each night. After the sermon, the preacher would declare that the doors of the church were open. This was the time for people to step forward and become members of the Body of Christ, one of three ways.

They could join by letter, which meant their current church home would certify that they were members in good standing; they could come on their Christian experience, which meant they had formerly belonged to a church but were no longer active; or they could come to be baptized.

The call to baptism proved irresistible to this unnamed church lady. She felt compelled to step forward and accept the Lord at just about every revival that came to town.

"I must have gotten myself baptized three or four times one summer before my mother told me once was enough," she reports.

Growing in faith, she has come to see the error of her youthful ways. She told me her story on the condition that I protect her identity.

I gave her my word.

Monkfish on the Grill

Monkfish has the flavor of lobster at a fraction of the cost. Grilling it on skewers makes for an impressive presentation.

MAKES 2–4 SERVINGS

Bamboo skewers for monkfish and
    vegetables
1 cup soy sauce
¼ cup balsamic vinegar
2 tablespoons Dijon mustard
½ cup chopped fresh flat-leaf parsley
¼ cup finely minced fresh ginger
3 cloves garlic, finely minced
½ cup orange juice with pulp
4 tablespoons sesame oil
1 pound monkfish or any firm-fleshed fish,
    cut into 2-inch cubes
1 Vidalia onion, cut into chunks
1 pound large mushrooms
1 eggplant, cut into 2-inch cubes
Salt and pepper to taste

Soak the skewers in water with 1 teaspoon of salt. In a small bowl, whisk together the soy sauce, vinegar, mustard, parsley, ginger, garlic, and orange juice. Drizzle in the sesame oil and continue whisking until well combined. Pour the mixture into a 9-by-13-inch baking dish. Thread the monkfish and vegetables on skewers, using two or three chunks of fish for each skewer. Place the skewers in the marinade, cover, and refrigerate for at least 2 hours, turning the skewers to be sure all the ingredients are well coated. Cook the skewers on a hot grill for 12 to 15 minutes or until fish is done, being careful not to overcook it. Heat the marinade in a small saucepan until it boils, then lower the heat and reduce the marinade by approximately half its volume. Serve the marinade as a sauce over the fish.

Note: Add red bell pepper pieces to the skewers for additional color.

—Brenda Rhodes Miller

Broiled Sea Bass

Just about any flaky, low-fat fish will taste delicious when prepared this way. Use fillets so that no one has to pick out the bones.

MAKES 4 SERVINGS

1 cup freshly squeezed lime juice
2 pounds sea bass fillets
Salt and pepper to taste
8 tablespoons (½ cup) butter

Preheat the oven to high broil. Rub ½ cup of the lime juice into the sea bass fillets and season them with salt and pepper to taste. Melt half the butter in a broiler pan, add the sea bass fillets, and dot with the remaining butter. Broil the fish on high about 4 minutes on one side; turn and broil another 3 to 4 minutes or until the fish is flaky. Remove the fish from the pan, stir the remaining lime juice into the pan drippings, and pour over the sea bass just before serving.

—Camille Samples

Grilled Tuna Steaks

Handle fresh tuna steaks as you would the most expensive cut of beef. Season them with care and never overcook them, because if you do, you'll ruin their wonderful flavor. Use that famous boxer's grill to cook tuna—never beyond medium. Teriyaki sauce gives the tuna a subtle flavor.

MAKES 4 SERVINGS

1 cup teriyaki sauce
¼ cup chopped garlic
2 tablespoons chopped fresh ginger
¼ cup canola oil
4 tuna steaks

Combine the teriyaki sauce, garlic, ginger, and oil in a blender. Marinade the tuna in the mixture for 1 hour. Heat a grill. Place the tuna steaks on the hot grill, sear one side, then turn to sear the other side. Remove from the heat and serve with a vegetable and either rice or potatoes.

—Millicent Bolden

Mama's Stuffed Red Snapper

This was one of my mother's favorite Sunday dinner dishes. Red snapper may be hard to find in some parts of the country, but you can substitute any other mild-flavored, nonoily fish. Have the fishmonger gut and clean the fish, leaving the head on. When I was a little girl, I couldn't bear the idea of the fish looking at me from the platter, so now I always cover the fish's eye with a lemon slice.

MAKES 4–6 SERVINGS

1 (4–6-pound) whole red snapper
2 tablespoons vegetable oil
2 whole lemons
½ cup diced celery
1 cup diced green bell pepper
1 cup diced red bell pepper
1½ cups diced onions
Salt and pepper to taste
5–6 round wooden toothpicks
1½ cups bottled salsa
Lemon wedges, for garnish

Preheat the oven to 375 degrees. Rub the inside and the outside of the fish with the oil, going from head to tail in the same direction as the scales. Be careful not to cut yourself on the bones and gills. Place the fish in a baking dish. Slice one lemon and line the inside of the fish with the lemon slices. Mix together the celery, peppers, onions, salt, and pepper and stuff the cavity of the fish. Secure with toothpicks or wooden kabob skewers and squeeze the remaining lemon over the fish. Bake about 50 minutes, or until the fish flakes when tested with a fork and the skin starts crisping. Top with the salsa and serve on a platter with lemon wedges.

—*Carolyn Bolden Rhodes*

Ce

Easy Seasoned Fried Catfish

If you have a favorite hot sauce, feel free to use it. Personally, I think Crystal Hot Sauce and fried fish were made for each other.

MAKES 6–8 SERVINGS

6 large catfish fillets, sliced about ½ inch
  thick
1–2 cups Crystal Hot Sauce, depending on
  the desired amount of spiciness
6 cups peanut oil
Seasoned fish-fry mix
Freshly squeezed lime juice (optional)

Place the catfish fillets in a sealable plastic bag. Pour in the hot sauce, seal the bag, and marinate in the refrigerator for several hours, turning the bag so all sides of the fish are

coated with sauce. When ready to fry, heat the oil in a cast-iron skillet. Remove the fillets from the marinade and dip them in the seasoned fish-fry mix. Place in the hot oil and fry until golden. Drain on paper towels. Dispose of the marinade; do not reuse it. Squeeze the lime juice over fillets before serving, if desired.

—*Dora Finley*

Ce

Salmon Loaf

Simple to prepare and tempting enough for even fussy eaters, this salmon loaf tastes good served hot or cold.

MAKES 4 SERVINGS

2 cups canned salmon, skin and bones
  removed
2 large eggs, well beaten
2 tablespoons butter, melted
½ cup white cornmeal
½ cup seasoned breadcrumbs
1 cup buttermilk
¾ cup cooked peas and carrots
Salt and pepper to taste
½ tablespoon vegetable oil

Preheat the oven to 425 degrees. Combine the salmon, eggs, butter, cornmeal, and bread crumbs in a large bowl. Stir in the buttermilk. Add the peas and carrots, season with salt and pepper if needed, and mix well. Pour the oil in the bottom of a 9-by-9-inch baking dish. Shape the salmon mixture into a loaf and place in baking dish. Bake for 15 minutes or until the salmon loaf is browned.

—Adapted from The Household Searchlight Recipe Book

What Is It About Death That Makes People So Chatty?

*f*ive minutes after a saint goes on to Glory, telephones start ringing off the wall. Bad news travels fast. And there are some church ladies who seem to feel it is their duty to spread the word.

Whether or not you are a friend of the deceased, whether or not you've ever met the dear departed, church ladies will certainly call to share the news that Mr. So-and-So has died. And then they'll do their level best to make you remember him, even if you have only the most tangential and remote of relationships.

"I know you met him. He was the great-uncle of the sister of the cousin on her mother's side of the guest preacher at the Spring Revival."

Polite people pretend to remember and solemnly offer the appropriate words of sympathy. To do any less would dishonor the suffering of the truly bereaved.

More painful, however, is when the deceased actually was a friend. What really hurts is when the news comes via a voice-mail message. *Blah blah blah. Blah blah blah* is how it sounds until the grief clears enough for the words to come through.

While it is always painful to learn of a friend's demise, the blow can be softened somewhat by the actual presence of a friend or relative to share the grief. As any good-hearted church lady will tell you, if you can't deliver sad news in person, by all means try to make sure the recipient is not alone when you say your piece.

After the initial flurry of phone calls, another round of calls heats up the lines as church ladies satisfy their morbid curiosity on the pretext of inquiring about "the arrangements" for the funeral.

Obviously, they can't ask the deceased any questions and most church ladies have the courtesy not to give surviving family members the third degree. With those constraints in mind, friends and acquaintances call on another to patch together bits of available information until the whole story emerges.

"What happened?" "Had he been sick long?" "I thought there was something wrong with her." "Was it sudden?" "When did you last see her?" "Did you know this was coming?" "How is the family holding up?"

There is a story behind every death, and friends will insist on telling it or having it told over and over again. Busybodies aside, however, most church ladies search for details as a way to help them make sense of death.

Belief in the Resurrection and everlasting life surely comfort the bereaved, but even women of faith must struggle with the pain of loss.

Church ladies share what they know about a death simply to reduce what is an unfathomable and mysterious reality into something more manageable.

When someone we know dies, the inevitability of our own deaths causes us talk and talk and then talk some more about how our friend came to pass away. At first all we can do is take stock of the immediate situation. So we talk about what happened and how it happened and what we could have, should have, but didn't do while we had time.

Rare is the death that does not call forth guilt, fear, and even shame among those left behind. Mercifully, however, those feelings tend to pass.

As time goes by, church lady friends begin to share stories of what the dear departed meant to them. They laugh together, cry together, and sometimes argue about what seems right and what seems wrong about the way things are going. They might critique the funeral and the behavior of the family. No matter. In their constant exchange of words, kind or cruel, loving or acrimonious, they reveal their basic humanity.

And that may be the best that any of us can do.

Salmon Cakes

Good for any meal or for appetizers if made silver-dollar size, salmon cakes are an easy way to introduce more fish into your diet.

MAKES 6–8 SERVINGS

1 (14.75-ounce) can salmon
1 large egg
4 tablespoons unflavored yogurt, mayonnaise, or sour cream
1/2 cup bread crumbs
3 teaspoons chopped fresh dill
Black pepper to taste
1 cup all-purpose flour, seasoned with salt and pepper, or fine cornmeal
Vegetable oil for frying
Lettuce leaves, for serving

Using a fork, mash the salmon, bones and all. In a medium bowl, lightly beat together the egg, yogurt, bread crumbs, dill, and pepper. Add the salmon and combine until the mixture holds together. Pat the mixture into cakes about 4 inches in diameter and dredge in the seasoned flour or cornmeal. Heat the oil in a large skillet, add the cakes, and brown on both sides over medium heat. Drain on newspaper covered with paper towels and serve on a bed of lettuce with tartar sauce or sweet mustard.

Note: Add 1/4 cup finely chopped celery to the salmon mixture for extra crunch.

—Brenda Rhodes Miller

Codfish Cakes

Dried, salted codfish has to be soaked in several changes of cold water to soften it up and remove the salt before it is ready to use. If you prefer, you can use canned codfish.

MAKES 4–6 SERVINGS

1/2 cup chopped celery
1/2 cup chopped green bell pepper
1/2 cup chopped green onions
2 cups cooked and mashed potatoes
1 1/2 cups codfish flakes
Black pepper to taste
1 large egg, beaten
1/2 cup all-purpose flour
Cooking oil

Combine the celery, bell pepper, and onions with the potatoes. Add the codfish, and season with the pepper. Stir in the beaten egg, blending well. Flour your hands, and shape the mixture into patties or balls. Lightly roll the cakes in the flour. Heat the cooking oil in a large skillet and fry the cod cakes until both sides are browned. Drain on newspaper covered with paper towels.

—Shirlene Archer

Seafood in Spicy Gravy the Easy Way

Use frozen crawfish meat, shrimp, crab, or calamari for this simple, but tasty, entrée. The main thing is to have plenty of fluffy rice to serve as the base. A salad is the only accompaniment you'll need.

MAKES 4 SERVINGS

2 ounces salt pork or bacon
2 tablespoons cooking oil
1 bunch chopped green onions
1 green bell pepper, chopped
1 large onion, chopped
2 cloves garlic, chopped
1 pound chopped crawfish meat, shrimp, crab, or calamari
1 (10½-ounce) jar chicken gravy
1 (8-ounce) bottle clam juice
½ tablespoon chopped fresh thyme
2 whole bay leaves
½ tablespoon red pepper flakes
4 cups cooked rice
¼ cup chopped fresh flat-leaf parsley

Chop the salt pork into 1-inch dice and fry them in a Dutch oven to release the fat. Add the cooking oil and sauté all vegetables in the oil mixture until they are soft. If using shrimp or calamari, add it now. Stir in the chicken gravy and clam juice. Add the thyme, bay leaves, and red pepper flakes. Add the craw-fish meat or crab, if using it. Cook on low heat for 10 minutes, taste, and adjust the seasonings. Simmer for 10 minutes longer. Serve in bowls over mounds of rice and topped with the fresh parsley.

—Lauren Cooper

Sinfully Simply Wonderful Scallops

The mistake most people make when they prepare scallops is to cook them until they're rubbery and tasteless. You can avoid that problem with this recipe.

MAKES 4 SERVINGS

1 pound fresh sea scallops (the big ones are sea scallops; the tiny ones are bay scallops)
¼ teaspoon salt
½–1 teaspoon pepper
½ teaspoon dried basil
1 tablespoon fine Italian bread crumbs
2 tablespoons olive oil
1 tablespoon butter
½ cup white cooking wine or seafood stock

Rinse the scallops and pat them dry. Put the scallops in a bowl and toss them with the salt, pepper, basil, and bread crumbs. In a heavy skillet, heat the olive oil and butter. When the

With a Song in Her Heart

LaCrechia Lyons
First Calvary Baptist Church
Knoxville, Tennessee

*L*aCrechia Lyons, first lady of First Calvary, freely admits that her favorite thing to do in the church is sing.

Currently, she directs both the Senior Choir and the Young Adult/Youth Choir, but she sings only with the Senior Choir. The average age of Senior Choir members is about sixty, and Mrs. Lyons reports that they appreciate her youthful soprano.

Her second most favorite thing to do in church is plan events. Every September her church celebrates Women's Month with a full series of activities, including a Luncheon and Fashion Show, a Women's Retreat in the mountains, and Christian outreach to a shelter for battered and abused women.

Bringing a spirit of encouragement to the women in the shelter, Mrs. Lyons and other church ladies serve them dinner and give them presents. They wrap and present thoughtful gifts such as nail polish and remover, scented lotions, bath salts, hair products, and other cosmetics and toiletries that offer the residents a way to pamper themselves despite their difficult circumstances.

As if these projects were not enough, Mrs. Lyons leads the Family Fellowship Ministry, which is responsible for running the annual Fall Festival, a big carnival within the church at which tickets are awarded for answering Bible trivia questions. Needless to say, the event is always packed—not only with church members but also neighbors living in the Lonsdale Homes, a housing development surrounding the church.

In addition, the Family Fellowship Ministry also presents a Christmas play or program and an annual Easter program. For yet another special program, members of the Ministry invite church ladies to come dressed as Bible characters.

Imagine if you can a room where Mary and Martha, Ruth and Naomi, Miriam and Salome, even Herod's and Pilate's wives gather to teach lessons from the Bible.

That must really be a sight to see.

butter begins to turn brown, place the scallops in the skillet. Cook the scallops on one side over medium-high heat until brown. Turn and cook on the other side. Remove the scallops from the skillet. Pour the cooking wine or seafood stock into the skillet and stir well to incorporate all the browned bits. Cook for about 2 minutes. This will make a sauce that is perfect served over Company Rice (page 000).

—*Camille Samples*

Ce

Fried Scallops and Crab Sticks

Crab sticks are not really crab but rather a fish mixture flavored to impersonate crab at a fraction of the cost. When fried, the crab sticks and scallops complement each other and make an impressive-looking platter.

MAKES 2 SERVINGS

1 large egg
Juice of ½ lemon
½ cup cold water
Seasoned salt, to taste
Seafood frying mix (flour or cornmeal based)
½ pound crab sticks
½ pound scallops
Peanut oil for frying

Whisk together the egg, lemon juice, cold water, and seasoned salt to make an egg wash. Pour about 1 cup of seafood frying mix onto a sheet of waxed paper. Remove the crab sticks from their plastic sleeves. Rinse the scallops and pat them dry. Toss the scallops and crab sticks in the egg wash. Place them on the seafood frying mix and lift the edges of the waxed paper to cover the seafood with the frying mix. Heat the peanut oil in a large skillet. Drop the seafood pieces in the hot oil and fry until golden brown. Drain on brown paper before serving.

—*Melanie Shelwood*

Ce

Shrimp in Spicy Tomato Sauce

Using bottled pasta sauce with vegetables cuts hours off this recipe. Add chopped green onions, green bell pepper, celery, extra garlic, and a bit of sage so the prepared sauce will cozy up to the shrimp in a special way.

MAKES 4 SERVINGS

¼ cup olive oil
4 cloves garlic, chopped
1 cup chopped green onions
½ cup chopped green bell pepper
½ cup chopped celery

1 (26-ounce) jar prepared pasta sauce with
    vegetables
1 pound shrimp, peeled and deveined
1 tablespoon chopped fresh sage
Salt and pepper to taste
3 cups cooked white rice

Heat the olive oil in a large skillet. Add the garlic, green onions, bell peppers, and celery, and sauté until the vegetables are soft. Pour the bottled pasta sauce over the vegetables, and stir well. Add the shrimp, sage, and salt and pepper to taste. Cook for 10 minutes. Serve over hot cooked rice.

—Leslie Williams

Pickled Shrimp

For a party more than twenty years ago, Pauline brought me a big bowl of her famous pickled shrimp set in a gaily decorated basket. What I took to be a gift tag tied to the handle with polka-dot ribbon turned out to be this recipe. Pauline instructed me to share her recipe with anyone at the party who asked for it. Serve Pauline's pickled shrimp on crisp lettuce with a few slices of ripe tomatoes and cheese wedges for a refreshing cold plate in summer. Be sure to devein the shrimp so your dish won't be gritty.

MAKES 4–6 SERVINGS

1 small Bermuda or other sweet onion, thinly
    sliced
3 cloves garlic, minced
1/4 teaspoon oregano
1/2 teaspoon fresh basil, finely shredded
1 bay leaf
1/4 teaspoon dry mustard
3 tablespoons freshly squeezed lemon juice
1/3–1/2 teaspoon sugar
1/4–1/2 teaspoon red pepper
4 tablespoons olive oil
1/2 cup red wine vinegar
1 1/2 pounds large shrimp, peeled and
    deveined, and cooked

Combine all the ingredients, except the shrimp, in a medium-sized glass bowl and mix well. Add the shrimp and mix well again. Cover and chill for at least 1 to 2 hours. Remove the bay leaf before serving on lettuce leaves with crusty bread for dipping in the sauce.

—Brenda Rhodes Miller

Garlicky Shrimp

I must admit to a bias for Gulf Coast shrimp, but shrimp from almost anywhere will pack powerful flavors when you use this easy recipe.

MAKES 8 SERVINGS

1 cup (2 sticks) butter, melted
1 cup olive oil
¼ cup minced garlic
¼ cup chopped fresh flat-leaf parsley
¼ cup minced chives
½ cup lemon juice
1 tablespoon hot sauce
Salt and pepper to taste
3 pounds shrimp, shelled and deveined

Preheat the oven to 425 degrees. Combine the melted butter, olive oil, garlic, parsley, chives, lemon juice, hot sauce, salt, and pepper in a large bowl. Taste and correct the seasonings. Add the shrimp and blend well. Place the shrimp mixture in a baking dish, and bake 3 to 5 minutes on one side; turn the shrimp, and bake 2 to 3 minutes on the other side. Remove from the baking dish and serve with the remaining pan sauce on the side and crusty bread.

Note: If you have any leftovers, toss with pasta for a quick, tasty supper.

—*Millicent Bolden*

Barbecued Shrimp

The name might lead you to believe that this shrimp dish is cooked on the grill. In fact, barbecued shrimp is really a shrimp dish baked in a hot and spicy sauce. Use head-on shrimp if you can get them because the flavor is exceptional.

MAKES 6–8 SERVINGS

2 cups hot sauce
½ cup minced garlic
1 cup olive oil
2 bay leaves, crumbled
1 cup (2 sticks) butter
½ cup chopped fresh oregano
¼ cup chopped fresh basil
½ cup freshly squeezed lemon juice
1 tablespoon salt
1 tablespoon celery salt
1 tablespoon sugar
2½ pounds shrimp, with heads, in their shells
1 loaf French bread

Preheat the oven to 400 degrees. Combine all the ingredients except the shrimp and French bread in a medium saucepan. Cook over medium heat, stirring constantly, until the ingredients are well blended. Put the shrimp in a 9-by-13-inch baking dish. Cover them with the sauce and toss to combine. Bake 15 to 20 minutes or until the shrimp turn bright pink. Serve with French bread for dipping in the sauce.

—*Melanie Shelwood*

Steamed Shellfish

Grocery store fish counters that steam shellfish while you wait may seem like a good idea—until they ruin your beautiful fresh seafood by over-cooking it. This do-it-yourself version takes only minutes and the mix lasts for ages.

MAKES 4–6 SERVINGS

1 cup salt
1 cup paprika
½ cup garlic powder
½ cup onion powder
6 bay leaves, crumbled
4 tablespoons celery seed
4 tablespoons red pepper flakes
¼ cup lemon-pepper seasoning
1 onion, peeled and cut in half
2 pounds large shrimp, in their shells
1 lemon, cut into wedges

Combine the first 8 ingredients on the list and store in an airtight container. Bring a pot of water to a rolling boil and add the onion. Put the shrimp in a colander and set it over the boiling water. Squeeze the juice from the lemon wedges over the shellfish and toss in the wedges. Sprinkle with 4 tablespoons of the seasoning mixture. Cover and cook for no more than 2 to 3 minutes or until the shrimp turn bright pink. Remove from the heat and pour ice water over the shrimp to stop their cooking. Serve with cocktail sauce, tartar sauce, or melted butter.

—Ben Cooper

Squash and Shrimp Casserole

This easy casserole is a good dish to bring to church suppers because it reheats well. It makes a filling main dish if you use equal amounts of squash and shrimp, and a light side dish if you reduce the quantity of shrimp.

MAKES 6–8 SERVINGS

Vegetable oil cooking spray
½ cup (8 tablespoons) butter or
 margarine
1½ pounds yellow squash, sliced thin
1 large onion, sliced thin
1½ pounds raw shrimp, peeled,
 deveined, and sliced in half
 lengthwise
¼–½ cup half-and-half or milk
1 cup shredded sharp Cheddar cheese
½ teaspoon paprika
¼ cup chopped fresh flat-leaf parsley
Dash of salt
½ cup unflavored bread crumbs

Preheat the oven to 425 degrees. Spray the bottom of a 9-by-12-inch baking dish with the cooking spray. Melt the butter in a large skillet, add the squash and onion, and sauté until tender. Turn off the heat, and stir in the shrimp. In a bowl, mix the half-and-half with the shredded cheese, paprika, parsley, and salt. Add the shrimp mixture, and blend well. Pour the ingredients into the prepared baking dish, top with the bread crumbs, and bake 30 to 45 minutes or until bubbly.

—Melanie Shelwood

Ce

Deviled Crab à la Lolita

East Coast crab cakes have their fans, but once you taste this spicy Gulf Coast dish you may become a convert. Deviled crabs look best when baked in real crab shells. Use a dull knife to remove the crab shell from a cooked crab. Scrape the inside of the shell. Soak the shells in hot water and vinegar to remove any leftover debris, then gently scrub them with a brush until clean. If you can find aluminum or ceramic crab shells, by all means use them instead of the real crab shells. Otherwise you can bake this in a glass baking dish.

MAKES 6 SERVINGS

1 cup diced celery

1½ cups diced green bell pepper

¾ cup diced yellow onion

½ cup (8 tablespoons) butter

1 roll Ritz crackers, crushed

3 eggs, lightly beaten

1 pound crab claw meat, picked clean of shell bits

1 tablespoon Worcestershire sauce

1 teaspoon seafood seasoning

Hot pepper sauce

2 tablespoons Dijon mustard

Parsley, for garnish

Sauté the celery, bell pepper, and onion in a large skillet in half the butter. Transfer the mixture to a large bowl and add half the cracker crumbs, the eggs, crabmeat, Worcestershire sauce, seafood seasoning, hot sauce, and mustard; mix well. Preheat the oven to 400 degrees. Butter six shells or six individual ramekins and fill with the crabmeat mixture. Sprinkle the remaining cracker crumbs on top and dot with the remaining butter. Bake 20 to 30 minutes or until heated and browned. Serve garnished with parsley.

—Mrs. Carolyn Lolita Bolden Rhodes

Ce

Crabs on the Grill

Use Dungeness, snow crab clusters, or dressed blue crabs in this recipe. A very hot fire guarantees that the crabs will cook quickly. Put a stick of butter in an ovenproof dish right on the grill so you'll have melted butter for dipping.

MAKES 4–6 SERVINGS

12 sprigs fresh thyme

2 cups olive oil

3 cloves garlic, crushed

5 pounds crab in the shell

½ cup (1 stick) butter

Chop 6 sprigs of the thyme. Combine the olive oil, chopped thyme, and garlic in a large bowl. Add the crabs to the bowl and rub the olive oil mixture into the shells and meat. Stick the remaining sprigs of thyme into the crabs. Put the butter in a heatproof pan and set in on a hot grill to melt. Add the crabs to the grill and cook 4 to 5 minutes, basting with the melted butter, until their shells turn red. Lower the grill temperature to medium-low, turn the crabs over, and baste again with the butter. Close the grill lid and cook 2 to 3 minutes or until the shells are slightly charred. Serve with mallets, cocktail forks, and crackers to get the meat from the shell. Use the remaining melted butter as a dipping sauce.

—Jay Cooper

Cee

Simple Stuffed Crabs

If your shellfish dishes never turn out quite right, you'll find that this recipe will change your luck. Use claw crabmeat because it is less expensive than lump crab and even more flavorful.

MAKES 6 SERVINGS

4 tablespoons (½ stick) butter
1 (10¾-ounce) can cream of mushroom soup
    or crab bisque
2 large eggs
1 pound claw crabmeat, imitation crabmeat,
    or canned crabmeat

¼ cup each chopped celery, green onions,
    and green bell pepper
1 cup unflavored bread crumbs

Preheat the oven to 400 degrees. Melt 1 tablespoon of the butter in each of 6 small ramekins. Beat the soup with the eggs in a medium bowl until smooth. Stir in the crabmeat, vegetables, and bread crumbs. Fill each ramekin about half full with crab mixture and bake about 15 minutes or until golden brown and puffy.

—Dora Finley

Cee

Easy Little Crab Omelets

Because these omelets are small, a little crabmeat will go a long way. Prepare the mixture in advance and refrigerate it until ready to serve.

MAKES 3–4 SERVINGS

6 large eggs
1 tablespoon whipping cream
Black pepper to taste
½ cup chopped green onions
¼ cup minced green bell pepper
¼ pound white lump crabmeat
Vegetable oil cooking spray

Whisk the eggs, cream, black pepper, and vegetables together in a large bowl. Gently fold in the crabmeat, taking care not to break up the lumps. Refrigerate for at least 1 hour or overnight if possible. To cook, spray a small skillet with cooking spray, and spoon about 2 tablespoons of omelet mixture into the pan. Cook on one side, then turn with a spatula and cook the other side. For a light supper, serve several omelets to each person, with fruit salad on the side.

—Dora Finley

Baked Clams

Overcooked clams and rubber bands are equally chewy. Use canned clams and clam juice for a melt-in-your-mouth taste of the sea.

MAKES 6–8 SERVINGS

4 strips bacon

1 cup finely chopped celery stalks and leaves

¼ cup chopped green onions

¼ cup minced fresh tarragon

¼ cup chopped fresh flat-leaf parsley

4 tablespoons (¼ cup) butter

1 cup Italian flavored bread crumbs

2 cups canned clams

1 (8-ounce) bottle clam juice

Preheat the oven to 350 degrees. Grease a 9-by-9-inch baking dish. Fry the bacon in a medium skillet until crisp. Remove the bacon, but do not drain the fat from the pan. Chop the bacon and set it aside. Sauté the celery and green onions in the bacon fat remaining in the pan. Add the tarragon, parsley, butter, and bread crumbs. Cook 5 minutes and remove from the heat. Stir in the clams, clam juice, and chopped bacon. Pour into the prepared baking dish and bake about 20 minutes.

—Jacqueline A. Duodu

Prayer Breakfast Dishes

Churches often hold prayer breakfasts as a way to combine two very important human enterprises: praying and eating in community. The recipes may be doubled as needed. Often, church ladies are willing to prepare their special breakfast dishes at home and bring them to church for sharing. Most of the recipes in this chapter make comforting and sustaining meals at any time of the day.

Come Ye Who Are Heavy Laden

COMFORTING THE BEREAVED

When an esteemed member of their community dies, African American church ladies immediately seek out ways to comfort the bereaved. Anybody with a lick of sense knows that even grieving people still have to eat. And since church ladies certainly have more than their fair share of good sense, food usually tops the list of condolences they offer the family.

There are usually at least one or two Honey Baked hams along with homemade potato salad and rolls. In addition, every grieving family receives several pound cakes, layer cakes with icing, roasted or smoked turkeys, fried and baked chicken, along with a variety of cooked vegetables and salads.

Other church ladies plan ahead for the days when the family's initial grieving period has ended. They bring dishes they have frozen and carefully labeled with reheating instructions for consumption at a later date. Comfort foods, such as chicken and dumplings, beef stew, meat loaf, roast beef with gravy, gumbo, chicken noodle soup, and every kind of casserole under the sun, are what they offer in lieu of flowers that nobody can eat anyway.

Since dinner isn't the only meal of the day, sometimes church ladies decide that when a family has lost a loved one baskets of breakfast foods are just what the doctor ordered. Peek into any such basket and you'll find boxes of cold cereal, muffins, instant oatmeal and grits, banana bread, bagels with cream cheese spreads, Danish pastries, jugs of orange juice, boxes of frozen waffles, jars of syrup, tubs of margarine or boxes of butter, slabs of country ham, cans of corned beef hash, packages of sausage, a dozen eggs, doughnuts, and maybe even a bag of coffee.

Melanie Shelwood is a church lady who works in the hospitality industry. Personal and professional experience has led her to reflect upon the art of bringing food gifts to bereaved families.

"The best thing people can do when they bring food to a family that has suffered a loss is to put their gifts in disposable pans so the family doesn't have to keep up with a lot of dishes that must be returned. But if someone decides to bring food in a dish she wants to get back, the thoughtful thing to do is to write your name on the bottom of the dish with an indelible ink pen."

Her advice doesn't stop there. "Regardless of what kind of dish you bring food in, and even if you don't have a sympathy card, just stick one of your address labels on a piece of paper or an index card. Jot down what you brought and attach it to the dish," she suggests. "When a family is already upset and stressed with grieving, it is hard for them to remember who brought what. Your preprinted address label on that card means they'll know what you brought and they won't have to search through a phone book for mailing information when it comes time to send a thank-you note."

Ms. Shelwood clearly expects that every family will thank those who offered them a kindness during their time of loss. She feels that sending a handwritten note is a gracious gesture. "People really appreciate a personal note, even though they do take more time to get done than ones with just a printed message," she says.

While food ranks as the most popular gift church ladies take to a grieving family, it isn't the only one. Providing paper plates, cups, and napkins are also thoughtful offerings and signal an understanding of the mourning family's state of mind by relieving them of having to do the dishes after every meal.

Church ladies who don't live in the same town as the bereaved family often tuck postage stamps into the condolence cards they send.

"We really appreciated the stamps some family friends sent when my mother died," Shelwood says. "Those stamps kept us from having to go to the post office and talking to strangers when we were already feeling very fragile. When we were ready to get our thank-you notes out, having the stamps on hand meant we could get the job done much faster."

While every expression of sympathy is deeply appreciated, there are some gifts that can really be tremendously helpful.

"Having a family friend volunteer to stay at the house during the funeral really helps a lot," says one who has reason to know. "People from out of town often call asking for directions, and it is a comfort to know that there is someone who will direct them to the church."

If small children are involved, their parents may decide not to have them attend the funeral. "It really helps for someone reliable to take charge of little children, amuse them and comfort them and keep them from worrying about where their parents are during the funeral. That's a real gift," says Shelwood.

The greatest gift of all, however, is having friends who stay in touch. "The funeral is not the end of grieving. It is just the beginning. The public, religious ceremony marking the passing of a loved one is hard, but the days after can be even harder.

"Our father died a few weeks before Father's Day. It meant everything that our friends and family stayed in touch with us that Sunday, on Daddy's birthday, and beyond. I don't know how we would have managed without their love and support." Church ladies show their innate kindness by making calls and sending notes for months after a death.

Even church ladies who have not suffered a personal loss share God's love by remembering the pain of others.

Fried Apples

Tart, crunchy apples cooked until soft and enlivened with sugar and spices are the ideal companion to bacon, sausage, ham, and even turkey. If you're strapped for time, use a mix of fresh and canned apples.

MAKES 2–4 SERVINGS

5 cups Granny Smith apples
5 tablespoons butter
1/2 cup granulated sugar
1/2 cup brown sugar
1 tablespoon apple pie spice
2 cups hot water
Dash of salt
Grated zest of 1 lemon

Wash, core, seed, but do not peel the apples and slice them in rounds. Melt the butter in a large skillet. Blend in the sugars and apple pie spice. Stir in the hot water to make a syrup. Reduce the heat and add the sliced apples and salt. Cook, covered, until the apples are soft, then stir in the lemon zest. Cook 5 minutes longer and serve.

—Millicent Bolden

Fruit Salad

Sweet, ripe summer fruits make the best salad. In the dead of winter you may have to rely on flash-frozen fruit thawed slowly in the refrigerator.

MAKES 6–8 SERVINGS

2 tablespoons honey
1 tablespoon balsamic vinegar or freshly
    squeezed lemon juice
6 cups watermelon balls
3 cups cantaloupe chunks
3 cups honeydew cubes
4 nectarines or peaches, peeled and sliced
2 kiwi fruits, peeled and sliced
1 pint berries of your choice
1 cup seedless grapes

Whisk together the honey and vinegar or lemon juice.

Place the fruit in a large bowl and pour the sauce over it. Serve immediately.

—Lauren Cooper

French Toast

Delicious French toast can be made with almost any bland, stale bread including white, wheat, French, or Italian breads. Stale bread soaks up the egg and milk mixture much better than fresh bread does. Keep a plastic bag in your freezer for leftover bread and bread ends to be thawed before making this recipe. Remember, the church ladies' mantra is "Waste not, want not."

MAKES 4–6 SERVINGS

10 to 12 slices stale bread
6 large eggs
3 cups whole milk or canned, evaporated
    milk
1/4 cup plus 2 teaspoons sugar
1 1/2 teaspoons vanilla
1 tablespoon cinnamon
1/2 cup butter
Jam, jelly, preserves, or syrup

Place a single layer of bread in a deep, flat dish. In a medium bowl, whisk together the eggs, milk, 2 teaspoons of the sugar, and the vanilla. Pour the mixture over the bread, piercing the slices with a fork so the bread absorbs the liquid. Turn once. Combine the remaining 1/4 cup of sugar with the cinnamon. Heat a large skillet or griddle and, when hot, coat it with the butter. Place the bread in the skillet or on the griddle and brown it on one side. Sprinkle the tops with the sugar and cinnamon mixture and turn the bread with a spatula to brown the other side. Sprinkle the second side with sugar and cinnamon and turn again to melt the sugar. Remove the bread and serve it with a dollop of jelly, jam, or preserves, or with syrup if you prefer.

—Brenda Rhodes Miller

Light-and-Cheesy Grits

The addition of beaten eggs and cheese to cooked grits provides a lighter but still rich and flavorful base for any other breakfast dish you might decide to serve.

MAKES 6–8 SERVINGS

1 (12-ounce) package grits
3 large eggs, beaten
1 cup shredded Cheddar cheese

Prepare the grits according to package directions. Combine the beaten eggs with the cheese. When the grits are almost done, add a few tablespoons of the hot grits to the egg and cheese mixture. Stir well to combine, then add the egg and cheese mixture to the cooked grits. Stir well, cover, and turn off the heat until ready to serve.

—Lolita Cusic

Grits and Gravy

Years ago, my friend and esteemed church lady, Delphine Smith, gave me a mug that read, "If you didn't want grits, why'd you order breakfast?" While it may be possible to hold a prayer breakfast without serving grits, what's the point?

MAKES 4 SERVINGS

1 (12-ounce) package instant grits
1 pound round steak
½ cup all-purpose flour
1 teaspoon salt
1 teaspoon black pepper
¼ teaspoon cayenne pepper
½ teaspoon garlic powder
½ teaspoon onion powder
½ cup vegetable oil
1 cup hot water
2 large eggs

Cook the grits according to package directions. Pound the round steak with a mallet until flat. Combine the flour, salt, peppers, and powders in a small bowl. Dredge the round steak with the flour mixture. Heat half the oil in a large skillet, and brown the round steak on both sides. Remove the steak from the pan and add the remaining oil and the flour mixture remaining in the bowl. Stir until the flour is browned. Add the hot water, stirring well until the gravy thickens. Return the meat to the gravy and cook, covered, on low. Just before serving, beat the eggs, and add some of the grits to eggs. Beat again and add the grits and egg mixture to the cooked grits. Stir well. Serve grits in a bowl with the meat on a platter and the gravy on the side.

—Brenda Rhodes Miller

Egg Surprise

Use this recipe to turn plain scrambled eggs into an attractive casserole. Rectangular baking dishes with their own wicker baskets and snap-on lids make it easy to transport the "surprise" any time of day.

MAKES 4 SERVINGS

2 bunches green onions, chopped
4 tablespoons olive oil
8 large eggs
1 cup chopped ham
1 cup shredded Cheddar cheese

Preheat the oven to 325 degrees. Grease a 9-by-9-inch baking dish. Sauté the green onions in the olive oil in a large skillet until fragrant. Beat the eggs and add them to the onions, stirring with a wooden spoon until the eggs reach the soft scrambled stage. Remove from the heat and stir in the chopped ham. Transfer the egg mixture to the prepared baking dish and cover with the shredded cheese. Bake 10 minutes or until the cheese melts.

—Mrs. Carolyn Lolita Bolden Rhodes

Flat Omelets

Surprise, surprise! Not every omelet has to be folded. If you've avoided trying to serve omelets because you couldn't quite master the fold, try this recipe. You can make this omelet in any size, depending on your frying pan, and then cut it into wedges to serve.

MAKES 4 SERVINGS

8 large eggs
Salt and pepper to taste
3 tablespoons olive oil
1 cup diced vegetables or meat or a
    combination of diced meat and vegetables
1/2 cup finely chopped fresh herbs
6 thin slices American or Cheddar cheese
    (optional)

Stir the eggs together with a fork. Add a little ice water and the salt and pepper. Heat the olive oil in a large skillet. Sauté the diced filling until the ingredients are tender. Pour in the beaten eggs and sprinkle the herbs over the mixture. With a fork, lift the edges of the cooked eggs so the raw egg mixture can run underneath. When the bottom is set, cover the skillet and continue cooking until the omelet is almost done. Place a large plate over the skillet and flip the eggs onto the plate. Slide the eggs back into the skillet and cover with the cheese, if using it. Re-cover the skillet and continue cooking until the eggs are firm. Slide the cooked omelet onto a plate, cut it into wedges, and serve.

Some interesting filling combinations include:

- Tomatoes, basil, and baby spinach or root onions

- Bell peppers and minced celery

- Parsley, thinly sliced garlic, and shallots

- Diced ham and cheese

- Minced shrimp, flaked, cooked fish, or diced chicken with tarragon

- Sautéed broccoli or a blend of your favorite fresh herbs

—Brenda Rhodes Miller

Judge Not Lest You Be Judged

MADELIENE DORIS DOUGLAS
LOS ANGELES, CALIFORNIA

In these increasingly uncivil times, some people think it's perfectly acceptable to take pot-shots at church ladies. The allegation of rampant hypocrisy is a favorite taunt of those who scoff at women's regular church attendance.

Parishioners of a certain Episcopal church on the West Coast were discussing this lamentable situation. Nodding heads and furrowed brows revealed the extent of their concern.

"I've heard people say the church is full of sinners. Why can't they understand the reason we come to church?"

After much give and take, one exuberant member proclaimed, "Of course we *are* all sinners. Yet we come asking for forgiveness. Church is where we come to improve. We are here because we are not all there yet."

True church ladies are the first to admit their own limitations. They do not pretend to be perfect because they know in their hearts they are "not all there yet."

By acknowledging their own faith journeys, church ladies constantly strive to be what God would have them to be.

There is no hypocrisy in that quest.

Mobile Breakfast Egg Casserole

Truly a one-dish meal to which all you may care to add are a fruit salad and perhaps some home-made biscuits.

MAKES 6–8 SERVINGS

1 cup chopped red bell pepper
1 cup chopped yellow onion
½ cup chopped celery leaves and stalks
1 large bay leaf
½ cup (1 stick) butter
2½ cups fresh or canned whole tomatoes, drained and coarsely chopped
1 cup seasoned bread crumbs
1½ pounds boneless, skinless whiting or cod fillets, cooked
1 pound sharp Cheddar cheese, grated
6 large eggs
Salt and pepper to taste

Preheat the oven to 350 degrees. Grease a 9-by-13-inch glass baking dish. In a medium skillet, sauté the bell pepper, onion, celery, and bay leaf in the butter for about 10 minutes. Remove the bay leaf; add the tomatoes and bread crumbs and mix well. Layer the vegetables in the bottom of the prepared baking dish. Break up the cooked fish fillets and spread them over the vegetables. Cover with a layer of the cheese, reserving some for the top. With the back of a spoon, make six depressions in the cheese. Crack an egg into each well, sprinkle with salt and pepper, and cover the eggs with the remaining cheese. Bake, covered, until the eggs are set and the cheese is melted.

—*Melanie Shelwood*

Easy-as-Pie Breakfast Bake

Serve this one-dish breakfast with Fried Apples (page 149) or Fruit Salad (page 150) for a complete meal. The only thing you need to add is a bunch of hungry people.

MAKES 4–6 SERVINGS

1 (8-count) can biscuits
½ pound cooked breakfast sausage
1 cup shredded Cheddar cheese

Preheat the oven to the temperature indicated on the biscuit can. Layer half of each biscuit in a pie pan. Add a layer of sliced sausage meat and sprinkle with the cheese. Top with the remaining biscuit dough and bake the biscuits according to the package directions. Serve with jam or jelly.

—*Leslie Williams*

Fried Oysters

In the Deep South, no Christmas breakfast is complete without a dish of grits and fried oysters. Small, salty oysters are preferred for morning meals.

MAKES 4 SERVINGS

1½ cups finely ground cornmeal
1 teaspoon paprika
1 teaspoon salt
1 teaspoon black pepper
½ teaspoon garlic powder
Dash of nutmeg
2 pints fresh oysters
2 large eggs, beaten with a tablespoon of cold
    water
8 cups peanut or canola oil

Combine the dry ingredients in a small bowl. Drain the oysters in a colander, reserving the liquid for soup or gumbo if you wish. Spread the dry ingredients on a large sheet of waxed paper. Dip the oysters in the egg mixture, then dredge them in the dry ingredients and turn to coat all sides. Heat the oil in a deep skillet and, when it is hot, slide the oysters into the skillet and fry until golden brown. Drain on a sheet of newspaper or brown paper covered with two sheets of paper towel. Serve with creamy grits for brunch or on French rolls for fried oyster sandwiches.

—Camille Sample

Tuna and Onions

Stock up on canned tuna when it goes on sale. That way you'll always have a versatile and economical main ingredient to use in this and other dishes.

MAKES 2–4 SERVINGS

1 (12-ounce) can oil-packed tuna
1 large onion, chopped
2 tablespoons butter
Black pepper to taste

Drain the tuna, reserving the oil. In a medium skillet, heat the tuna oil and the butter. Add the onion and cook until golden. Add the tuna and the black pepper and cook until heated through. Serve with grits and bran muffins.

—Mrs. Carolyn Loita Bolden Rhodes

Esther T. Hall. Anne M. Roberson, Jacqueline A. Horton, and Gwendolyn Lang are all members of the Good Samaritans Club in Toulminville-Warren United Methodist Church. They comfort the bereaved with friendly smiles and a hearty repast.

CHAPTER 9

Desserts, Beverages,

and Sauces

Done Paid My Vow to the Lord and I Never Will Turn Back.
I Will Go. I Shall Go to See What the End May Be.

CHURCH LADIES ON FIDELITY

Fidelity is a fine old word that has lost much of its meaning. With the possible exception of the Marine Corps, which uses fidelity as its rallying cry, the only time fidelity is ever mentioned these days seems to be in the context of marriage.

According to Webster's dictionary, fidelity is "careful observance of duty, or discharge of obligations." The root word for fidelity is *faith*.

When one joins a church or belongs to a particular religious denomination, one vows to uphold the tenets of that faith. And, while membership does indeed have its privileges, it also comes with definite obligations.

We regularly recite creeds or covenants during the worship service to remind us of what we have promised God. But, regardless of what they do in God's service, church ladies always base their actions on faith.

What better word than fidelity is there to describe why it is that church ladies act as living witnesses within their respective congregations? The concept of devotion to duty is often discredited in modern life. "Do what you want" has replaced the concept of doing what you must. But church ladies believe that being faithful to their obligations and vows is a noble calling.

To do so, however, one must have a clear understanding of what those vows and obligations really mean. Unfortunately, people often get confused. And perhaps nowhere is that confusion more obvious than in the identification of the role of godparents.

Whatever the denomination, every child who is baptized, christened, or dedicated in a religious ceremony has godparents. Usually a man and a woman who have an emotional or familial investment in the child will stand with the parents during the service. Most of the time those people are also church members, meaning that one of them is sure to be a church lady.

Being a godparent is a serious commitment. Godparents are charged with supporting the parents in the religious education of the child. This can mean being the person who makes sure the child attends Sunday school even if the parents do not or cannot. It may also include talking to the child about God and providing opportunities for worship and religious instruction.

Far too many otherwise intelligent parents believe that when they select godparents, they are also providing guardians for their child in case of their own death. However, being a godparent is not the same as being a legal guardian. It is indeed a prudent course of action for parents to ask for, get approval from, and complete the legal arrangements to identify the adults who will be responsible for their children should the parents die. But determining a prospective legal guardian is not at all the same thing as picking godparents.

Sacramental obligations and legal obligations are totally different. While parents may select the same people to fulfill both duties, there are distinct procedures for institutionalizing the sacred duties separate and apart from the legal duties.

Fidelity is the basis of a godparent's commitment. When you ask a church lady to stand as godparent to a child, she will most willingly strive to do her Christian duty. That's why it is vital to be clear from the outset what you are asking.

I grew up in the United Methodist Church. When I was christened—my church being one that believed in infant baptism—my parents selected family friends to be my godparents. Their names are written in my baby book. The fading ink is silent testimony to their faithful devotion.

"Your mother and daddy were at our house playing cards. All of us were eating hot dogs because schoolteachers didn't make enough money to serve anything else. When they left after midnight, your mother was complaining of indigestion. Early the next morning our telephone rang, and it was your daddy telling us you'd arrived. We couldn't believe it because they'd just left us and you weren't due for another three weeks." My godfather delights in telling this story.

As I moved though confirmation and Methodist Youth Fellowship, my godparents remained involved in my religious education. To this day, they are active participants in my life.

Did my parents expect my godparents to act as surrogate parents in the event of their deaths? I doubt it. But they did expect fidelity from the friends they trusted with the religious education of their baby girl.

They were never disappointed.

Cu

The Easiest Bread Pudding on the Planet

Bread pudding is a super-easy dessert even when it's made from scratch. But it's especially easy when you use eggnog as the main ingredient. If you like raisins or currants, add a cup to the recipe. If you don't like nuts, leave them out.

MAKES 12 SERVINGS

8 cups stale bread or stale pound cake
1/2 cup (1 stick) butter
3 large eggs
1 cup sugar
2 teaspoons vanilla

1 quart eggnog
1 tablespoon ground cinnamon
1 1/2 teaspoons ground nutmeg
1 1/2 teaspoons ground ginger
1/4 cup grated orange rind
1 1/2 cups chopped pecans or walnuts

Preheat the oven to 350 degrees. Cut the stale bread or pound cake into chunks and set it aside. Put the butter in a 3-quart baking dish and put the dish in the oven to melt the butter. When the butter has melted, add the bread chunks to the dish and combine them with the melted butter, stirring to coat them well. In a large bowl, whisk together the eggs and sugar. Whisk in the vanilla. Add the eggnog in a steady stream, whisking well. Whisk in the spices, then stir in the orange rind and pecans. Pour the mixture into the baking dish and press down until all the liquid has been soaked up by the bread or pound cake. Bake 1 hour or until golden brown on top.

—Brenda Rhodes Miller

Cu

Banana Pudding

Whether you prefer boxed vanilla pudding, homemade custard, or this easy condensed-milk version from Mrs. Joyce Clemons, banana pudding is a classic. Use very ripe bananas because they are extra sweet. After you slice the bananas, cover them with a little pineapple juice so they don't turn brown. The pineapple juice will also add extra zip.

MAKES 6–8 SERVINGS

1 (12-ounce) box vanilla wafers

6 ripe bananas

½ cup pineapple juice

1 (14-ounce) can sweetened condensed milk

½ cup half-and-half

3 large eggs, separated

1½ teaspoons vanilla

½ cup confectioners' sugar

4 tablespoons (¼ stick) butter

Preheat the oven to 400 degrees. Grease a 3-quart baking dish. Line the bottom and sides of the baking dish with vanilla wafers. Slice the bananas into ½-inch-thick rounds. Place the sliced bananas in a zip-top bag with the pineapple juice, seal the bag, and shake to coat all the banana slices with juice. Pour the condensed milk, half-and-half, egg yolks, and vanilla into a bowl and beat until thoroughly combined. Place a layer of bananas over the vanilla wafers in the baking dish. Spread a layer of the egg yolk mixture over the bananas. Add another layer of vanilla wafers. Continue layering bananas, wafers, and egg yolk mixture until the dish is full. Beat the egg whites in a cold bowl with the confectioners' sugar and a few tablespoons of the pineapple juice until stiff peaks form to make a meringue. Spoon the meringue over top of the banana pudding, swirling to make peaks. Bake until the meringue is lightly browned, which will also cook the egg yolks in the pudding. Cool slightly before serving.

—Joyce Clemons

Easy Cranberry Peach Cobbler

Any brand of boxed baking mix, such as Bisquick, can be used to make Lauren Cooper's simple cobbler, which has a cake-like texture and a pleasing flavor.

MAKES 8 SERVINGS

½ cup butter

1 cup fresh cranberries

1 cup sugar

3 large eggs

2 cups baking mix

1 (5-ounce) can evaporated milk

1 (29-ounce) can sliced cling peaches in heavy syrup, drained, syrup reserved

1 quart vanilla ice cream

Preheat the oven to 350 degrees. Place the butter in a 2-quart baking dish and melt it in the oven. Increase the oven temperature to 375 degrees. Rinse the cranberries in a colan-

Meet the Seven Women in Hats

MRS. RITA HARDY THOMPSON
NEW REDEEMER BAPTIST CHURCH
WASHINGTON, D.C.

Should you ever get invited to a program titled "Seven Women in Hats," you'd best know your stuff. As one of the featured church ladies, you'll have to make a short speech about your duties and role within the church, complete with biblical references.

Mrs. Rita Thompson, the first lady of her church, recently held such an event at New Redeemer. Each speaker brought a contingent of other church ladies with her. And, of course, they were all encouraged to wear their grandest hats.

The Seven Women in Hats included church ladies from the Trustee Ministry, the Usher Board, and the Sunday school ministry. There was also a deaconess, a church clerk, a missionary, and, of course, a first lady. All were women renowned for their service to the church.

Four judges from New Redeemer faced the daunting challenge of judging a hat contest, which every woman wearing a hat entered automatically. Categories included the biggest, the smallest, the most flamboyant, and the most colorful hats.

If you've ever seen the vast array of hats worn by African American church ladies, you'll have some idea of how difficult judging such a contest can be.

Mrs. Thompson herself owns all kinds of hats. Her favorite is a big black and white summer straw hat. It has a nautical look and matches a suit she enjoys wearing.

This stylish summer straw seems the perfect choice for the proud mother of a Naval Academy graduate who is now an officer in the U.S. Navy.

And she wears it well.

der, discarding any mushy or blighted berries. Place the cranberries in a small bowl, cover them with the sugar, and stir to coat. In a medium bowl, whisk together the eggs, baking mix, ½ cup of the peach syrup, and the milk until well blended. Add the melted butter and mix well. Pour the mixture into the baking dish. Drop the peaches and cranberries into the mixture. Do not stir. Bake 40 minutes or until the mixture rises above the fruit and browns. Serve warm with scoops of vanilla ice cream.

—Lauren Cooper

Cee

Aunt Dot's Pound Cake

This recipe is so easy that even a novice baker is guaranteed good results. My aunt Dot always used cake flour, but sifted all-purpose flour works well too.

MAKES 16–18 SERVINGS

1 (8-ounce) package cream cheese, softened
1½ cups butter, softened
3 cups sugar
6 large eggs
1 teaspoon vanilla
2 teaspoons lemon extract
3 cups cake flour or sifted all-purpose flour

Preheat the oven to 300 degrees. Grease and flour a 12-cup tube pan. In a large bowl, beat the cream cheese and butter together with the sugar until light and fluffy. Add the eggs, vanilla, and lemon extract and blend until smooth. Stir in the flour, and beat until the batter is well mixed. Pour into the tube pan and bake for 1½ hours or until a toothpick inserted in the center comes out clean. Cool

slightly on a wire rack, then remove from pan and cool completely. Serve plain or with fresh fruit or ice cream as an added treat.

—Mrs. Bessie Brazley

Cee

Brown Sugar Pound Cake

Marshel O'Shields gave me this recipe after I spoke at the George Mason Library in Fairfax, Virginia *The Church Ladies' Divine Desserts* had brought forth memories of his daughter's birthday cake of choice. Her parents mailed one to her each of the four years she was away at college, with varying degrees of success. After she graduated and moved to Alabama, they found a baker in the town where she lived and asked him if he could bake the cake for her. He agreed to give it a try if they would send the recipe. When he had baked and delivered the cake, he liked the results so much that he didn't charge the parents for doing it!

MAKES 18–20 SERVINGS

1 cup vegetable shortening
½ cup butter
1 pound light brown sugar
5 large eggs
3 cups sifted all-purpose flour
½ teaspoon salt
¾ teaspoon baking powder
1 cup evaporated milk

1 or 2 teaspoons vanilla
2 teaspoons maple flavoring
Brown Sugar Cake Frosting (recipe follows)

Preheat the oven to 300 degrees. Grease and flour a 12-cup tube pan. Cream the shortening, butter, and sugar together in a large bowl. Add the eggs, one at a time, beating well after each addition. Resift the flour with the salt and baking powder. Add the flour and milk alternatively to the creamed mixture. Stir in the vanilla and maple flavoring. Pour the cake batter into the prepared pan and bake for 1½ hours or until a toothpick inserted in the center of the cake comes out clean. Cool before frosting.

BROWN SUGAR CAKE FROSTING
½ cup butter
1 cup packed light brown sugar
½ cup evaporated milk
1 pound confectioners' sugar
1 teaspoon vanilla

Melt the butter, stir in the brown sugar, and cook 1 minute. Cool slightly and add the evaporated milk. When the mixture has cooled completely, add the confectioners' sugar and vanilla and beat well.

—Marshel O'Shields

Garden of Eden Cake

The cardinal rule of all good church ladies is "Waste not, want not." This recipe is a good reason to keep pieces of stale angel food cake on hand in your freezer.

MAKES 6–8 SERVINGS

1 angel food cake
2 cups canned tropical fruit or plain fruit cocktail or any combination of canned fruits
1 (3-ounce) package vanilla instant pudding

Break up the cake into crumbs. Drain the fruit, and use the liquid to prepare the pudding according to package directions. In a square 9-inch baking dish, layer the cake crumbs and fruit. Pour prepared pudding over the cake and fruit. Warm slightly before serving.

—Mrs. Rubye Smith Bull

Tang Pie

The old standby powdered juice mix takes on new life in this easy no-bake pie. The filling can be made with either orange or green Tang for variety.

MAKES 16 SERVINGS

Pray Without Ceasing

MRS. MARIA DE SILVA
ST. PATRICK'S CATHOLIC CHURCH
PROVIDENCE, RHODE ISLAND

You might not expect a person who made bayonets and other kinds of knives during World War II to be a bona fide church lady today. That's because you don't know Mrs. Maria de Silva.

Her Cape Verdean heritage is the reason she can speak Portuguese. Her love of God is the reason she is now a Charismatic Catholic.

Charismatic Catholics believe in direct and immediate divine inspiration, which they see manifested in healing, speaking in tongues, prophesizing, and other spiritual gifts.

While Mrs. de Silva has been Catholic all her life, she only became a Charismatic Catholic about twenty years ago, during a time of great personal travail when she recalls crying every day into her supper.

Mrs. Maria de Silva enjoying conversation before a fellowship meal at St. Patrick's Catholic Church in Providence, Rhode Island.

Despite her own suffering, she couldn't help but notice that some members of her immediate family seemed exceptionally calm and happy. One day her son asked her if she was born again and invited her to go to church with him.

"The church met in a basement. I went and I cried and cried. It was a cleansing kind of crying. They say God comes to your heart and cleans it out."

She prayed and asked God to show her what to do. Then she began attending a Charismatic Church with her sister-in-law.

"The Holy Spirit was really strong. I could hear the prophecies. I could feel the Word really touch me."

She continued praying, asking God to touch her through her husband who, she admits, was not much for going to church.

"But he went three times in a row. That was my sign to become Charismatic." Today she and her husband take up the collection each Sunday. "Sometimes things happen that bring you to the Lord. Things happen that change your heart."

½ cup orange or green Tang

1 (5-ounce) can sweetened condensed milk

1 cup sour cream

2 cups frozen dessert topping, such as Cool
    Whip, thawed

2 Cookie Crumb Piecrusts (page 165) or
    2 graham cracker piecrusts

1 (8-ounce) can mandarin orange slices or
    1 small lime, sliced thin

Mix the Tang, milk, sour cream, and whipped topping in a medium bowl and pour into the pie shells. Chill until ready to serve. You may garnish the orange Tang pie with well-drained slices of mandarin orange. For the green Tang pie, curl the lime slices and arrange around the rim of the pie.

Variation: Instead of pouring the filling into the piecrusts, layer it with crumbled cream-filled chocolate cookies in tall parfait glasses.

—LaVerne Finley

Ce

Cookie Crumb Piecrust

This recipe gives you a sweet foundation for your pie filling. Try several combinations of cookie crumbs and fillings to discover your favorite.

MAKES 1 (9-INCH) PIE CRUST

2 cups crumbled cookies, such as chocolate or
    vanilla wafers, gingersnaps, or sandwich
    cookies*

½ stick melted butter

Preheat the oven to 400 degrees. Combine cookie crumbs and melted butter and press the mixture into the bottom and sides of a pie pan. Bake 10 minutes. Cool before filling.

—Camille Samples

*To crumble the cookies, put them in a blender and pulse until they are crushed to fine crumbs. If using sandwich cookies, reduce the amount of butter slightly. The filling will hold the crumbs together with just a little butter.

Ce

Sweet Potato Pie

Holiday dinner wouldn't be complete without an old-fashioned sweet potato pie. Once you've made this one, I guarantee it will become a family staple.

MAKES 12–14 SERVINGS

5 large baked sweet potatoes, peeled and
    mashed

4 large eggs

½ cup half-and-half

1 cup sugar

1 teaspoon vanilla

¾ teaspoon nutmeg

½ teaspoon cinnamon

½ cup (1 stick) butter, melted

2 (9-inch) deep-dish piecrusts

Preheat the oven to 350 degrees. Beat the sweet potatoes in a large bowl with the eggs, half-and-half, sugar, vanilla, spices, and melted

Suffer the Little Children—to Celebrate

MRS. RUBYE SMITH BULL
ST. AUGUSTINE EPISCOPAL CHURCH
ST. PETERSBURG, FLORIDA

Mrs. Rubye Smith Bull is a great lady. Gracious to a fault, she is known for her warm and embracing personality. Her smile offers instant welcome, and she is generous with her time and energy. Plus, she knows how to have fun.

Years ago, when her granddaughter turned five, Mrs. Bull and her daughter, the little girl's mother, gave a cookie party to celebrate the grand occasion. As the guests arrived, Mrs. Bull covered their party dresses with lovely handmade aprons, managing to tie perfect bows at the waists of fifteen squirming five-year-olds.

"I cut out every one of those little aprons all by myself," Mrs. Bull recalls. "Then I went over to my girlfriend's house so she could help me put on the sashes. We added some lace and rickrack trim for decoration. I don't think we even hemmed the aprons, there were so many of them."

As you can imagine, the little girls were thrilled. They welcomed Mrs. Bull into their midst, and she soon became the life of the birthday party.

With Mrs. Bull as her able assistant, the "cookie teacher," who had been hired for the occasion, showed the girls how to measure and sift, how to use a mixer and a rolling pin. Mrs. Bull threw herself into baking with such gusto that the little girls were swept along by her enthusiasm.

Because of her, they were brave, those little bakers, venturing into territory unknown to most five year-olds. They tried all the cookie cutter shapes and used sprinkles of every color on their finished products.

Instead of the traditional goody bag, each child went away with a batch of homemade cookies nestled in beribboned cellophane to share with her parents. Before leaving, they hugged and kissed Mrs. Bull, and several of them made sure to invite her to their own birthday parties.

butter until well blended. Taste and adjust the spices. Pour the mixture into the pie shells and bake 30 to 35 minutes or until the filling is set and the shells are golden brown. Remove from the oven and cool on wire racks. Serve either warm or refrigerated.

—Shirlene Archer

Ce

Bountiful Harvest Pie

The year Shelley Fleming planted zucchini, her harvest was so abundant that she shared the bounty with all her friends and even provided recipes.

MAKES 8 SERVINGS

*6½ cups tender, young zucchini, peeled,
    seeded, and sliced ¼ inch thick*
½ teaspoon vanilla extract
2 sheets prepared pastry dough
¾ cup granulated sugar
¾ cup packed light brown sugar
1½ teaspoons cinnamon
½ teaspoon nutmeg
1½ teaspoons cream of tartar
2 tablespoons cornstarch
½ teaspoon salt
¼ cup butter
1 teaspoon apple cider vinegar

Cook the zucchini for 2 minutes in boiling water. Drain in a colander. Add the vanilla and refrigerate for at least an hour. Preheat the oven to 475 degrees. Grease a pie plate, then line it with 1 sheet of pastry dough. In a medium bowl, lightly combine the chilled zucchini, granulated sugar, brown sugar, cinnamon, nutmeg, cream of tartar, cornstarch, and salt. Fill the pie plate with the zucchini mixture. Dot the filling with butter (reserving some for the crust) and pour the vinegar over the top. Cover with the second sheet of pastry dough and crimp the edges to seal them. Prick the surface with a fork in several places and dot the top crust with tiny chunks of the remaining butter. Bake for 10 minutes, then reduce the oven temperature to 350 degrees and bake for approximately 1 hour 15 minutes longer.

—Shelley Fleming
    Adapted from Hometown Recipes from
    Dolly Massaro

Ce

Impossible-to-Ruin Dessert for Dummies

It's almost impossible to ruin this dessert. You can make it all year long with whatever fruit is at its peak of ripeness. Or you can use frozen or dried fruit. Just be sure to lay a piece of foil under the dish in case of spillovers in the oven.

MAKES 4–6 SERVINGS

5 cups sliced fresh fruit in season

1 cup all-purpose flour

1/8 teaspoon salt

1 cup sugar

1 tablespoon baking powder

1 large egg

3/4 cup evaporated milk or half-and-half

1 tablespoon grated orange or lemon rind

6 tablespoons butter, melted

1 quart vanilla ice cream

Preheat the oven to 350 degrees. Grease a 9-inch baking dish. Layer the sliced fruit on the bottom of the baking dish. Sift together the

---

Spiritual Gifts

LaVerne Finley
St. Edmonds by the Sea Catholic Church
Dauphin Island, Alabama

Even church ladies in the know tend to forget that hospitality is actually an important spiritual gift, ranking right up there with teaching, administration, and healing. Indeed, there is now a school of thought that views the story of Sodom and Gomorrah through the lens of hospitality. That's powerful stuff.

LaVerne Finley understands the value of hospitality. She warmly welcomes guests to her home in Jackson, Mississippi, where she shares not only Southern hospitality but also true Christian fellowship.

Her primary ministry as a church lady is to work with teens who are pregnant or parents. Married at a young age herself, she has a special understanding and profound compassion for the special challenges teenage parents face.

Praiseworthy work indeed, but that is only a fraction of what she does. She unselfishly opens her home to those who suffer and are brokenhearted. Her ministry extends to applying the balm of hospitality to wounded souls. But she offers the same gracious hospitality to everyone. She frequently invites friends to a beautiful family retreat on the Gulf of Mexico where the sound of waves and the cawing of seagulls provide a welcome respite from the frantic noisiness of twenty-first-century life.

And by so doing, she gives living witness to her faith.

---

flour, salt, sugar, and baking powder. In a medium bowl, beat the egg with the milk, the grated orange peel, and the melted butter. Add the liquid mixture to the dry ingredients and blend well. Pour the mixture over the fruit and bake for 35 to 40 minutes. A crust will form on top of the fruit, and it should be nicely browned when the dessert is done. Serve with scoops of vanilla ice cream.

—Marshel O'Shields

Ce

Cherry Float

This recipe comes from Marshel O'Shields's mother-in-law, Mrs. Paul Houston. According to Marshel, it is just *good!*

MAKES 6–8 SERVINGS

2 cups all-purpose flour
2 teaspoons baking powder
½ teaspoon salt
1½ cups sugar
2 tablespoons vegetable shortening
⅔ cup milk
2 cups canned cherries, drained, juice reserved
Whipped cream, for serving (optional)

Preheat the oven to 350 degrees. Grease a 10-by-15-inch baking dish with butter. Sift together the flour, baking powder, salt, and ½ cup of the sugar. Crumble the shortening into the above ingredients and add the milk, stirring

well. Pour the mixture into the prepared baking dish and cover with the cherries. Sprinkle the remaining 1 cup of sugar over the cherries. Measure the reserved cherry juice and add enough hot water to make 2 cups. Pour the liquid over the ingredients in the pan and bake 45 minutes or until browned and bubbly. Serve with a dollop of whipped cream, if desired.

—Marshel O'Shields

Ce

Fruit Delight

Use either Granny Smith apples or firm pears in this recipe. Even hard plums will work if that's what you have on hand.

MAKES 6–8 SERVINGS

5–6 cups sliced Granny Smith apples, firm
pears, or hard plums, or a mixture of these
fruits
½–¾ cup granulated sugar
½ cup packed light brown sugar
1 cup whole-wheat flour, stirred to remove
lumps
¼ teaspoon nutmeg
¼ teaspoon ginger
¼ teaspoon cinnamon
1 teaspoon baking powder
¾ teaspoon salt
3 small or 2 large eggs
⅓ cup melted butter
Whipped cream, for serving (optional)

Preheat the oven to 350 degrees. Grease a 9-inch baking dish. Place the sliced fruit on the bottom of the baking dish. In a bowl, use a fork to combine all the remaining ingredients except the melted butter. Sprinkle the mixture over the sliced fruits and drizzle the butter over the topping. Bake 30 to 40 minutes. Serve with whipped cream, if desired.

—Marshel O'Shields

In the Fullness of Time

MARSHEL O'SHIELDS
FALLS CHURCH, VIRGINIA

Under the best of circumstances, fruitcakes present strange and mysterious challenges. Both preparation and storage require a single-minded dedication. Butter-rich batter full of candied fruit and nuts, cheesecloth veils and repeated dousing with bourbon or rum all set fruitcakes apart, as does the labor involved in making them. The fruit must be floured lest it sink to the bottom of the batter. Fruitcakes have to be wrapped and sprinkled and turned for several weeks before they can be served. The rules go on and on.

Ordinary cake protocol tends not to apply to these substantial holiday offerings. Do you know anyone who has ever asked for a *second* slice of fruitcake?

Some would even go so far as to relegate fruitcakes to the status of bookends and doorstops. The six or seven people in the country who enjoy fruitcake cry, "Shame on them."

Marshel O'Shields's mother always managed to burn her fruitcakes at Christmastime due to the vagaries of her oven, until, in 1953, she finally got a new oven with a timer. Young Marshel was certain this would "fix" her problem, and he carefully set the timer for his mother so it would go off just exactly when specified by the recipe.

Fruitcakes take quite a while to bake. The timer went off and the cakes rested in the cooling oven. It should have worked like a charm.

Except. Except. Except. When the elder Mr. O'Shields got up the next morning, he decided to make himself a couple of slices of cheese toast for breakfast.

Without opening the oven, he set it to preheat on broil so his cheese would melt. The poor fruitcakes burned again.

Ma Hamlin's Peanut Sweeties

Peanuts add both crunch and flavor to these delicious little cookies. Be sure not to grind them too long or you'll get peanut butter instead of peanut crumbs.

MAKES ABOUT 4 DOZEN

1 cup butter
½ cup granulated sugar
½ cup packed light brown sugar
3 cups all-purpose flour, sifted
1 cup ground peanuts
3 tablespoons milk, as needed
1 cup peanut butter chips
1 cup confectioners' sugar

Cream the butter and sugars until fluffy. Add the flour and beat until smooth. Stir in the ground peanuts. If mixture seems too stiff, add the milk, 1 tablespoon at a time, stirring well. Roll the dough into a ball, wrap it in plastic, and refrigerate for 1 hour or overnight. Preheat the oven to 350 degrees. With floured hands, pinch off pieces of dough (about 1 tablespoon per cookie). Flatten the dough slightly and put a few peanut butter chips in the middle, then pinch the edges together to make a small ball. Place the cookies on an ungreased baking sheet as they're formed. Bake 10 minutes or until the dough is golden brown. Sift the powdered confectioners' sugar over the cookies while they're still warm.

—Mrs. Blanche Hamlin

Easy Dessert Topping

Prepared puddings, whether chocolate, vanilla, or butterscotch, can turn store-bought, unfrosted cake into a company-worthy dessert. Since this is dessert, do not use the no-fat varieties.

MAKES 1 CUP TOPPING

2 (4-ounce) cups prepared pudding, your
    choice of flavor
½ teaspoon nutmeg for vanilla-flavored
    pudding
2 teaspoons raspberry jam for chocolate-
    flavored pudding
1 teaspoon rum-flavored extract for
    butterscotch pudding
1 store-bought, unfrosted Bundt cake,
    cut into wedges
½ cup sliced berries of your choice

Spoon the pudding of your choice into a small bowl. Whisk in the specified addition, spoon the pudding over the cake, and garnish each wedge with a few berries.

—Lauren Cooper

Smooth Lemon Sauce

Set off your favorite bread or rice pudding recipe by topping it with this simple sauce. The alcohol cooks off, leaving a tasty lemon and bourbon flavor.

MAKES ABOUT 1¼ CUPS SAUCE

1 (9-ounce) jar lemon curd
2 tablespoons bourbon
1 tablespoon butter

Spoon the lemon curd into a small saucepan. Add the butter and bourbon and cook over low heat until the butter melts and the lemon curd liquefies. Stir well to blend. Serve drizzled over individual servings of bread pudding or rice pudding.

—Brenda Rhodes Miller

Ce

Mint Iced Tea

Just about the only thing more refreshing than cold sweet tea is that same tea flavored with fresh mint. Plant some mint now so you'll have plenty when the hot weather comes.

MAKES 18–20 SERVINGS

8 cups water
12 tea bags
12 sprigs fresh mint, plus additional for garnish

6 large lemons
2 cups sugar
10 cups cold water

Boil the 8 cups of water in a medium saucepan. Remove from the heat and add the tea bags and 5 sprigs of the mint. Cover and let stand for 20 minutes. Cut up the lemons and combine them with the sugar, crushing the lemons into the sugar to release their flavor. Add the remaining 7 sprigs of mint and crush them into the lemon mixture.

Cover the lemon and sugar mixture with 10 cups of cold water and let stand for 15 minutes. Pour the tea and mint mixture through a strainer into a pitcher. Add the lemon, sugar, and mint mixture and stir to combine. Serve in tall glasses filled with crushed ice. Garnish each glass with a sprig of mint.

—Adapted from Secrets of Southern Maryland Cooking: How to Keep Daddy Home

Ce

Miss Rena's Iced Tea Drink

Although nothing can match iced tea as a refreshing summertime beverage, it is also a year-round church meal staple.

MAKES 6 SERVINGS

1 quart tea
Sugar to taste
Juice of 1 lemon
1 pint ginger ale
Tea Cubes (recipe follows)

Combine the first four ingredients in a pitcher and stir well. Serve over Tea Cubes.

Tea Cubes

Make 4 cups iced tea and sweeten to taste. Pour into ice cube trays and freeze. Once frozen, remove from the trays and store in a sealable plastic bag in the freezer to use when you make iced tea so the flavor is not diluted by plain ice cubes.

—Rena Simmons

Orange Blossom Tea

The light flavor of oranges makes this a perfect beverage for a ladies' tea. It is equally delicious served cold. Orange-flower water is a flavoring for pastries and beverages that can be found in specialty shops and some liquor stores.

MAKES 12–16 SERVINGS

3 cups sugar
1 cup orange juice
1 cup orange-flower water

1 gallon strong hot tea
1 orange, sliced very thin

Add the sugar, orange juice, and orange-flower water to the hot tea and stir to mix.

Place a single slice of orange in a teacup and pour the tea over it. Serve hot or over ice.

—Brenda Rhodes Miller

'Nita's Punch

My cousin Juanita Eaton is famous for serving this refreshing and fruity punch. It tastes best when made in advance so the flavors have a chance to mellow.

MAKES 1 GALLON

1 (3-ounce) box lime-flavored gelatin
2 cups sugar
2 cups hot water
3 cups cold water
1 (46-ounce) can pineapple juice
1 (8-ounce) bottle lemon juice
1 (1-ounce) bottle almond flavoring
2 liters ginger ale, lemon-lime soda, or ginger beer

Combine the gelatin, sugar, and hot water in a medium bowl. Add the cold water, pineapple juice, lemon juice, and almond flavoring and stir well to combine. Place in a covered container and store in a cool place for no more than one or two days. When ready to serve, add the ginger ale, lemon-lime soda, or ginger beer.

—*Juanita Eaton*

Ce

Wedding Punch

Frozen sugared rose petals add a lovely touch to this punch, making it the ideal beverage for weddings and other celebrations.

MAKES 10–12 SERVINGS

8 tablespoons confectioners' sugar
2 cups water
1 cup culinary rose petals that have not been
  sprayed with pesticides
1 cup granulated sugar
½ cup freshly squeezed lemon juice
2 (24-ounce) bottles sparkling cider, chilled
2 cups rose water, chilled

Combine 6 tablespoons of the confectioners' sugar with the 2 cups water. Pour the sugar water into 4½-cup plastic containers. Add the rose petals and freeze. Mix the granulated sugar and the lemon juice in a punch bowl. Pour the sparkling cider and rose water over the lemon and sugar mixture. Stir well. Add the frozen sugared rose petals just before serving. Dust the rim of the punch bowl with the remaining 2 tablespoons of confectioners' sugar.

—*Melanie Shelwood*

Fruit Salsa

Sweet, ripe fruit is essential to this recipe. Serve the salsa with grilled chicken, grilled fish, or pork roast for a tropical main dish.

3 tablespoons freshly squeezed lime juice
1 tablespoon peanut oil
1 cup nectarines, peeled and finely
  chopped
2 medium jalapeño peppers, seeded
  and diced
3 green onions, chopped fine
1 cup diced fresh or canned pineapple
½ cup diced cantaloupe
½ red bell pepper, chopped fine
1 tablespoon minced cilantro

Whisk the lime juice and oil together in a small bowl. In a glass bowl, combine all the remaining ingredients. Pour the lime juice mixture over the other ingredients, mix lightly, and refrigerate until ready to serve.

—*Lauren Cooper*

Ce

Cruzan Barbecue Sauce

Molasses and rum have long been kissing cousins in the Americas. Each is a by-product of sugar production that begins with the harvesting of sugar cane. Both commodities figured prominently in the slave trade and, as such, are an important part of African American history. Teetotalers need not worry, as the alcohol burns off when the rum is heated.

MAKES 5 CUPS SAUCE

2 (8-ounce) bottles prepared barbecue sauce
1 cup pineapple juice
1 cup rum
1 cup molasses

Pour the barbecue sauce in a saucepan. Add the remaining ingredients, tasting and adding more of one or another until the flavor suits you. Warm the sauce briefly over low heat.

Use the sauce to baste chicken or ribs on the grill.

Contributors

Shirlene Archer
Ava Blocker
Millicent Bolden
Wiley L. Bolden
Gracie Brigs
Bessie Brazlay
Maretta Brown-Miller
Rubye Smith Bull
Vina Mae Carroll
Martha Chubb
Joyce Clemons
Priscilla Coatney
William Coatney
Luevenia Combest
Sameka Cook
Ben Cooper
Jay Cooper
Lauren Cooper
Sara Garcia Cooper
Shawn Cooper
Beverly Crandall
Edythe Crump
Lolita Cusic
Phillip Cusic
Maria de Silva
Madeliene Doris Douglas
Jacqueline A. Duodu
Juanita Eaton

Joyce Felder
Dora Finley
La Verne Finley
Alene Fleming
Shelley Fleming
Candace Grigsby
Esther T. Hall
Blanche Hamlin
Dorothy I. Height
Jacqueline A. Horton
Beulah Hughes
Geneva Jackson
Janet Jamieson
Martha Jamieson
Troy Johnston
Joyce Ladner
Gwendolyn Lang
LaCrechia Lyons
Carol Martin
Joyce McCannon
Timothy F. Merkel
Alyce Miller
Clarence Earl Miller
Courtenay L. Miller
Flora J. Moore
Lorraine Moore
Marshel O'Shields
Johnnie Overton

Anne Anderson Paulin
Libba Pendleton
Adah E. Pierce
Dian M. Powell
Melvin Powell
Carolyn Lolita Bolden Rhodes
Charles Rhodes
Lottie Twyner Rhodes
Anne M. Roberson
Ellen Robinson
Camille Samples
Ruby Saunders
Mrs. Cornell Sharperson
Melanie Shelwood
Rena Simmons
Virginia Strong
Annetta Maria Thomas
Evelyn Thompson
Rita Hardy Thompson
Sharon Thurman
Abigail Walker
Carrie White
Cynthia Williams
Leslie Williams
Ruth E. Willis
Tyrone Wise
Fannie Wortham

The Books

Mobile Twyners' Favorite Recipes
Compiled by Juanita Eaton
Family Reunion, August 1991

Hometown Recipes
From Dolly Massaro

The Household Searchlight Recipe Book
Capper Publications, Inc.
Topeka, Kansas, 1944

Secrets of Southern Maryland Cooking: How
to Keep Daddy Home
Charles County Children's Aid Society, Inc.
La Plata, Maryland, 1954

A Dash of Sevillity
Pensacola Heritage Foundation, Florida 1971

Beard on Bread
Alfred Knopf
New York 1980

Index